BRAVE NEW WORLD

Aldous Huxley

INTRODUCTION:
STOPPING TO BUY SPARKNOTES ON A SNOWY EVENING

Whose words these are you *think* you know.
Your paper's due tomorrow, though;
We're glad to see you stopping here
To get some help before you go.

Lost your course? You'll find it here.
Face tests and essays without fear.
Between the words, good grades at stake:
Get great results throughout the year.

Once school bells caused your heart to quake
As teachers circled each mistake.
Use SparkNotes and no longer weep,
Ace every single test you take.

Yes, books are lovely, dark, and deep,
But only what you grasp you keep,
With hours to go before you sleep,
With hours to go before you sleep.

CONTENTS

Context

ALDOUS HUXLEY WAS BORN in Surrey, England on July 26, 1894 to an illustrious family deeply rooted in England's literary and scientific tradition. Huxley's father, Leonard Huxley, was the son of Thomas Henry Huxley, a well-known biologist who gained the nickname "Darwin's bulldog" for championing Charles Darwin's evolutionary ideas. His mother, Julia Arnold, was related to the important nineteenth-century poet and essayist Matthew Arnold.

Raised in this family of scientists, writers, and teachers (his father was a writer and teacher, and his mother a schoolmistress), Huxley received an excellent education, first at home, then at Eton, providing him with access to numerous fields of knowledge. Huxley was an avid student, and during his lifetime he was renowned as a generalist, an intellectual who had mastered the use of the English language but was also informed about cutting-edge developments in science and other fields. Although much of his scientific understanding was superficial—he was easily convinced of findings that remained somewhat on the fringe of mainstream science—his education at the intersection of science and literature allowed him to integrate current scientific findings into his novels and essays in a way that few other writers of his time were able to do.

Aside from his education, another major influence on Huxley's life and writing was an eye disease contracted in his teenage years that left him almost blind. As a teenager Huxley had dreamed about becoming a doctor, but the degeneration of his eyesight prevented him from pursuing his chosen career. It also severely restricted the activities he could pursue. Because of his near blindness, he depended heavily on his first wife, Maria, to take care of him. Blindness and vision are motifs that permeate much of Huxley's writing.

After graduating from Oxford in 1916, Huxley began to make a name for himself writing satirical pieces about the British upper class. Though these writings were skillful and gained Huxley an audience and literary name, they were generally considered to offer little depth beyond their lightweight criticisms of social manners. Huxley continued to write prolifically, working as an essayist and journalist, and publishing four volumes of poetry before beginning to work on novels. Without giving up his other writing, beginning in

1921, Huxley produced a series of novels at an astonishing rate: *Crome Yellow* was published in 1921, followed by *Antic Hay* in 1923, *Those Barren Leaves* in 1925, and *Point Counter Point* in 1928. During these years, Huxley left his early satires behind and became more interested in writing about subjects with deeper philosophical and ethical significance. Much of his work deals with the conflict between the interests of the individual and society, often focusing on the problem of self-realization within the context of social responsibility. These themes reached their zenith in Huxley's *Brave New World,* published in 1932. His most enduring work imagined a fictional future in which free will and individuality have been sacrificed in deference to complete social stability.

Brave New World marked a step in a new direction for Huxley, combining his skill for satire with his fascination with science to create a dystopian (anti-utopian) world in which a totalitarian government controlled society by the use of science and technology. Through its exploration of the pitfalls of linking science, technology, and politics, and its argument that such a link will likely reduce human individuality, *Brave New World* deals with similar themes as George Orwell's famous novel *1984.* Orwell wrote his novel in 1949, after the dangers of totalitarian governments had been played out to tragic effect in World War II, and during the great struggle of the Cold War and the arms race which so powerfully underlined the role of technology in the modern world. Huxley anticipated all of these developments. Hitler came to power in Germany a year after the publication of *Brave New World.* World War II broke out six years after. The atomic bomb was dropped thirteen years after its publication, initiating the Cold War and what President Eisenhower referred to as a frightening buildup of the "military-industrial complex." Huxley's novel seems, in many ways, to prophesize the major themes and struggles that dominated life and debate in the second half of the twentieth century, and continue to dominate it in the twenty-first.

After publishing *Brave New World,* Huxley continued to live in England, making frequent journeys to Italy. In 1937 Huxley moved to California. An ardent pacificist, he had become alarmed at the growing military buildup in Europe, and determined to remove himself from the possibility of war. Already famous as a writer of novels and essays, he tried to make a living as a screenwriter. He had little success. Huxley never seemed to grasp the requirements of the form, and his erudite literary style did not translate well to the screen.

In the late forties, Huxley started to experiment with hallucinogenic drugs such as LSD and mescaline. He also maintained an interest in occult phenomena, such as hypnotism, séances, and other activities occupying the border between science and mysticism. Huxley's experiments with drugs led him to write several books that had profound influences on the sixties counterculture. The book he wrote about his experiences with mescaline, *The Doors of Perception,* influenced a young man named Jim Morrison and his friends, and they named the band they formed The Doors. (The phrase, "the doors of perception" comes from a William Blake poem called *The Marriage of Heaven and Hell.*) In his last major work, *Island,* published in 1962, Huxley describes a doomed utopia called Pala that serves as a contrast to his earlier vision of dystopia. A central aspect of Pala's ideal culture is the use of a hallucinogenic drug called "moksha," which provides an interesting context in which to view *soma,* the drug in *Brave New World* that serves as one tool of the totalitarian state. Huxley died on November 22, 1963, in Los Angeles.

UTOPIAS AND DYSTOPIAS

Brave New World belongs to the genre of utopian literature. A utopia is an imaginary society organized to create ideal conditions for human beings, eliminating hatred, pain, neglect, and all of the other evils of the world.

The word utopia comes from Sir Thomas More's novel *Utopia* (1516), and it is derived from Greek roots that could be translated to mean either "good place" or "no place." Books that include descriptions of utopian societies were written long before More's novel, however. Plato's *Republic* is a prime example. Sometimes the societies described are meant to represent the perfect society, but sometimes utopias are created to satirize existing societies, or simply to speculate about what life might be like under different conditions. In the 1920s, just before *Brave New World* was written, a number of bitterly satirical novels were written to describe the horrors of a planned or totalitarian society. The societies they describe are called dystopias, places where things are badly awry. Either term, utopia or dystopia, could correctly be used to describe *Brave New World*.

PLOT OVERVIEW

THE NOVEL OPENS in the Central London Hatching and Conditioning Centre, where the Director of the Hatchery and one of his assistants, Henry Foster, are giving a tour to a group of boys. The boys learn about the Bokanovsky and Podsnap Processes that allow the Hatchery to produce thousands of nearly identical human embryos. During the gestation period the embryos travel in bottles along a conveyor belt through a factorylike building, and are conditioned to belong to one of five castes: Alpha, Beta, Gamma, Delta, or Epsilon. The Alpha embryos are destined to become the leaders and thinkers of the World State. Each of the succeeding castes is conditioned to be slightly less physically and intellectually impressive. The Epsilons, stunted and stupefied by oxygen deprivation and chemical treatments, are destined to perform menial labor. Lenina Crowne, an employee at the factory, describes to the boys how she vaccinates embryos destined for tropical climates.

The Director then leads the boys to the Nursery, where they observe a group of Delta infants being reprogrammed to dislike books and flowers. The Director explains that this conditioning helps to make Deltas docile and eager consumers. He then tells the boys about the "hypnopaedic" (sleep-teaching) methods used to teach children the morals of the World State. In a room where older children are napping, a whispering voice is heard repeating a lesson in "Elementary Class Consciousness."

Outside, the Director shows the boys hundreds of naked children engaged in sexual play and games like "Centrifugal Bumble-puppy." Mustapha Mond, one of the ten World Controllers, introduces himself to the boys and begins to explain the history of the World State, focusing on the State's successful efforts to remove strong emotions, desires, and human relationships from society. Meanwhile, inside the Hatchery, Lenina chats in the bathroom with Fanny Crowne about her relationship with Henry Foster. Fanny chides Lenina for going out with Henry almost exclusively for four months, and Lenina admits she is attracted to the strange, somewhat funny-looking Bernard Marx. In another part of the Hatchery, Bernard is enraged when he overhears a conversation between Henry and the Assistant Predestinator about "having" Lenina.

After work, Lenina tells Bernard that she would be happy to accompany him on the trip to the Savage Reservation in New Mexico to which he had invited her. Bernard, overjoyed but embarrassed, flies a helicopter to meet a friend of his, Helmholtz Watson. He and Helmholtz discuss their dissatisfaction with the World State. Bernard is primarily disgruntled because he is too small and weak for his caste; Helmholtz is unhappy because he is too intelligent for his job writing hypnopaedic phrases. In the next few days, Bernard asks his superior, the Director, for permission to visit the Reservation. The Director launches into a story about a visit to the Reservation he had made with a woman twenty years earlier. During a storm, he tells Bernard, the woman was lost and never recovered. Finally, he gives Bernard the permit, and Bernard and Lenina depart for the Reservation, where they get another permit from the Warden. Before heading into the Reservation, Bernard calls Helmholtz and learns that the Director has grown weary of what he sees as Bernard's difficult and unsocial behavior and is planning to exile Bernard to Iceland when he returns. Bernard is angry and distraught, but decides to head into the Reservation anyway.

On the Reservation, Lenina and Bernard are shocked to see its aged and ill residents; no one in the World State has visible signs of aging. They witness a religious ritual in which a young man is whipped, and find it abhorrent. After the ritual they meet John, a fair-skinned young man who is isolated from the rest of the village. John tells Bernard about his childhood as the son of a woman named Linda who was rescued by the villagers some twenty years ago. Bernard realizes that Linda is almost certainly the woman mentioned by the Director. Talking to John, he learns that Linda was ostracized because of her willingness to sleep with all the men in the village, and that as a result John was raised in isolation from the rest of the village. John explains that he learned to read using a book called *The Chemical and Bacteriological Conditioning of the Embryo* and *The Complete Works of Shakespeare,* the latter given to Linda by one of her lovers, Popé. John tells Bernard that he is eager to see the "Other Place"—the "brave new world" that his mother has told him so much about. Bernard invites him to return to the World State with him. John agrees but insists that Linda be allowed to come as well.

While Lenina, disgusted with the Reservation, takes enough *soma* to knock her out for eighteen hours, Bernard flies to Santa Fe where he calls Mustapha Mond and receives permission to bring

John and Linda back to the World State. Meanwhile, John breaks into the house where Lenina is lying intoxicated and unconscious, and barely suppresses his desire to touch her. Bernard, Lenina, John, and Linda fly to the World State, where the Director is waiting to exile Bernard in front of his Alpha coworkers. But Bernard turns the tables by introducing John and Linda. The shame of being a "father"—the very word makes the onlookers laugh nervously—causes the Director to resign, leaving Bernard free to remain in London.

John becomes a hit with London society because of his strange life led on the Reservation. But while touring the factories and schools of the World State, John becomes increasingly disturbed by the society that he sees. His sexual attraction to Lenina remains, but he desires more than simple lust, and he finds himself terribly confused. In the process, he also confuses Lenina, who wonders why John does not wish to have sex with her. As the discoverer and guardian of the "Savage," Bernard also becomes popular. He quickly takes advantage of his new status, sleeping with many women and hosting dinner parties with important guests, most of whom dislike Bernard but are willing to placate him if it means they get to meet John. One night John refuses to meet the guests, including the Arch-Community-Songster, and Bernard's social standing plummets.

After Bernard introduces them, John and Helmholtz quickly take to each other. John reads Helmholtz parts of *Romeo and Juliet,* but Helmholtz cannot keep himself from laughing at a serious passage about love, marriage, and parents—ideas that are ridiculous, almost scatological in World State culture.

Fueled by his strange behavior, Lenina becomes obsessed with John, refusing Henry's invitation to see a feely. She takes *soma* and visits John at Bernard's apartment, where she hopes to seduce him. But John responds to her advances with curses, blows, and lines from Shakespeare. She retreats to the bathroom while he fields a phone call in which he learns that Linda, who has been on permanent *soma*-holiday since her return, is about to die. At the Hospital for the Dying he watches her die while a group of lower-caste boys receiving their "death conditioning" wonder why she is so unattractive. The boys are simply curious, but John becomes enraged. After Linda dies, John meets a group of Delta clones who are receiving their *soma* ration. He tries to convince them to revolt, throwing the *soma* out the window, and a riot results. Bernard and Helmholtz, hearing of the riot, rush to the scene and come to John's aid. After the riot is calmed by police with *soma* vapor, John, Helmholtz, and Bernard are arrested and brought to the office of Mustapha Mond.

John and Mond debate the value of the World State's policies, John arguing that they dehumanize the residents of the World State and Mond arguing that stability and happiness are more important than humanity. Mond explains that social stability has required the sacrifice of art, science, and religion. John protests that, without these things, human life is not worth living. Bernard reacts wildly when Mond says that he and Helmholtz will be exiled to distant islands, and he is carried from the room. Helmholtz accepts the exile readily, thinking it will give him a chance to write, and soon follows Bernard out of the room. John and Mond continue their conversation. They discuss religion and the use of *soma* to control negative emotions and social harmony.

John bids Helmholtz and Bernard good-bye. Refused the option of following them to the islands by Mond, he retreats to a lighthouse in the countryside where he gardens and attempts to purify himself by self-flagellation. Curious World State citizens soon catch him in the act, and reporters descend on the lighthouse to film news reports and a feely. After the feely, hordes of people descend on the lighthouse and demand that John whip himself. Lenina comes and approaches John with her arms open. John reacts by brandishing his whip and screaming "Kill it! Kill it!" The intensity of the scene causes an orgy in which John takes part. The next morning he wakes up and, overcome with anger and sadness at his submission to World State society, hangs himself.

CHARACTER LIST

John The son of the Director and Linda, John is the only major character to have grown up outside of the World State. The consummate outsider, he has spent his life alienated from his village on the New Mexico Savage Reservation, and he finds himself similarly unable to fit in to World State society. His entire worldview is based on his knowledge of Shakespeare's plays, which he can quote with great facility.

Bernard Marx An Alpha male who fails to fit in because of his inferior physical stature. He holds unorthodox beliefs about sexual relationships, sports, and community events. His insecurity about his size and status makes him discontented with the World State. Bernard's surname recalls Karl Marx, the nineteenth-century German author best known for writing Capital, a monumental critique of capitalist society. Unlike his famous namesake, Bernard's discontent stems from his frustrated desire to fit into his own society, rather than from a systematic or philosophical criticism of it. When threatened, Bernard can be petty and cruel.

Helmholtz Watson An Alpha lecturer at the College of Emotional Engineering, Helmholtz is a prime example of his caste, but feels that his work is empty and meaningless and would like to use his writing abilities for something more meaningful. He and Bernard are friends because they find common ground in their discontent with the World State, but Helmholtz's criticisms of the World State are more philosophical and intellectual than Bernard's more petty complaints. As a result, Helmholtz often finds Bernard's boastfulness and cowardice tedious.

Lenina Crowne A vaccination worker at the Central London Hatchery and Conditioning Centre. She is an object of desire for a number of major and minor characters, including Bernard Marx and John. Her behavior is sometimes intriguingly unorthodox, which makes her attractive to the reader. For example, she defies her culture's conventions by dating one man exclusively for several months, she is attracted to Bernard—the misfit—and she develops a violent passion for John the Savage. Ultimately, her values are those of a conventional World State citizen: her primary means of relating to other people is through sex, and she is unable to share Bernard's disaffection or to comprehend John's alternate system of values.

Mustapha Mond The Resident World Controller of Western Europe, one of only ten World Controllers. He was once an ambitious, young scientist performing illicit research. When his work was discovered, he was given the choice of going into exile or training to become a World Controller. He chose to give up science, and now he censors scientific discoveries and exiles people for unorthodox beliefs. He also keeps a collection of forbidden literature in his safe, including Shakespeare and religious writings. The name Mond means "world," and Mond is indeed the most powerful character in the world of this novel.

Fanny Crowne Lenina Crowne's friend (they have the same last name because only about ten thousand last names are in use in the World State). Fanny's role is mainly to voice the conventional values of her caste and society. Specifically, she warns Lenina that she should have more men in her life because it looks bad to concentrate on one man for too long.

Henry Foster One of Lenina's many lovers, he is a perfectly conventional Alpha male, casually discussing Lenina's body with his coworkers. His success with Lenina, and his casual attitude about it, infuriate the jealous Bernard.

Linda John's mother, and a Beta. While visiting the New
Mexico Savage Reservation, she became pregnant with
the Director's son. During a storm, she got lost,
suffered a head injury and was left behind. A group of
Indians found her and brought her to their village.
Linda could not get an abortion on the Reservation,
and she was too ashamed to return to the World State
with a baby. Her World State–conditioned promiscuity
makes her a social outcast. She is desperate to return to
the World State and to *soma*.

The Director The Director administrates the Central London
Hatchery and Conditioning Centre. He is a threatening
figure, with the power to exile Bernard to Iceland. But
he is secretly vulnerable because he fathered a child
(John), a scandalous and obscene act in the World
State.

The Arch-Community-Songster The Arch-Community-
Songster is the secular, shallow equivalent of an
archbishop in the World State society.

Popé Popé was Linda's lover on the New Mexico Savage
Reservation. He gave Linda a copy of *The Complete
Works of Shakespeare*.

The Warden The Warden is the talkative chief administrator for
the New Mexico Savage Reservation. He is an Alpha.

ANALYSIS OF MAJOR CHARACTERS

JOHN

Although Bernard Marx is the primary character in *Brave New World* up until his visit with Lenina to the Reservation, after that point he fades into the background and John becomes the central protagonist. John first enters the story as he expresses an interest in participating in the Indian religious ritual from which Bernard and Lenina recoil. John's desire first marks him as an outsider among the Indians, since he is not allowed to participate in their ritual. It also demonstrates the huge cultural divide between him and World State society, since Bernard and Lenina see the tribal ritual as disgusting. John becomes the central character of the novel because, rejected both by the "savage" Indian culture and the "civilized" World State culture, he is the ultimate outsider.

As an outsider, John takes his values from a more than 900-year-old author, William Shakespeare. John's extensive knowledge of Shakespeare's works serves him in several important ways: it enables him to verbalize his own complex emotions and reactions, it provides him with a framework from which to criticize World State values, and it provides him with language that allows him to hold his own against the formidable rhetorical skill of Mustapha Mond during their confrontation. (On the other hand, John's insistence on viewing the world through Shakespearean eyes sometimes blinds him to the reality of other characters, notably Lenina, who, in his mind, is alternately a heroine and a "strumpet," neither of which label is quite appropriate to her.) Shakespeare embodies all of the human and humanitarian values that have been abandoned in the World State. John's rejection of the shallow happiness of the World State, his inability to reconcile his love and lust for Lenina, and even his eventual suicide all reflect themes from Shakespeare. He is himself a Shakespearean character in a world where any poetry that does not sell a product is prohibited.

John's naïve optimism about the World State, expressed in the words from *The Tempest* that constitute the novel's title, is crushed when he comes into direct contact with the State. The phrase "brave new world" takes on an increasingly bitter, ironic, and pessimistic tone as he becomes more knowledgeable about the State. John's participation in the final orgy and his suicide at the end of the novel can be seen as the result of an insanity created by the fundamental conflict between his values and the reality of the world around him.

BERNARD MARX

Up until his visit to the Reservation and the introduction of John, Bernard Marx is the central figure of the novel. Bernard's first appearance in the novel is highly ironic. Just as the Director finishes his explanation of how the World State has successfully eliminated lovesickness, and everything that goes along with frustrated desire, Huxley gives us our first glimpse into a character's private thoughts, and that character is lovesick, jealous, and fiercely angry at his sexual rivals. Thus, while Bernard is not exactly heroic (and he becomes even less so as the novel progresses), he is still interesting to the reader because he is human. He wants things that he can't have.

The major movement in Bernard's character is his rise in popularity after the trip to the Reservation and his discovery of John, followed by his disastrous fall. Before and during his trip to the Reservation, Bernard is lonely, insecure, and isolated. When he returns with John, he uses his newfound popularity to participate in all of the aspects of World State society that he had previously criticized, such as promiscuous sex. This about-face proves Bernard to be a critic whose deepest desire is to become what he criticizes. When John refuses to become a tool in Bernard's attempt to remain popular, Bernard's success collapses instantaneously. By continuing to criticize the World State while reveling in its "pleasant vices," Bernard reveals himself to be a hypocrite. John and Helmholtz are sympathetic to him because they agree that the World State needs criticizing and because they recognize that Bernard is trapped in a body to which his conditioning has not suited him, but they have no respect for him. Lenina's relationship to Bernard is different: she sees him merely as a strange, interesting fellow with whom she can take a break from her relationship with Henry Foster. She is happy to use him for her own social gain, but she doesn't have the emotional investment in him that she does in John.

HELMHOLTZ WATSON

Helmholtz Watson is not as fully developed as some of the other characters, acting instead as a foil for Bernard and John. For Bernard, Helmholtz is everything Bernard wishes he could be: strong, intelligent, and attractive. As such a figure of strength, Helmholtz is very comfortable in his caste. Unlike Bernard, he is well liked and respected. Though he and Bernard share a dislike of the World State, Helmholtz condemns it for radically different reasons. Bernard dislikes the State because he is too weak to fit the social position he has been assigned; Helmholtz because he is too strong. Helmholtz can see and feel how the shallow culture in which he lives is stifling him.

Helmholtz is also a foil for John, but in a different way. Helmholtz and John are very similar in spirit; both love poetry, and both are intelligent and critical of the World State. But there is an enormous cultural gap between them. Even when Helmholtz sees the genius in Shakespeare's poetry, he cannot help but laugh at the mention of mothers, fathers, and marriage—concepts that are vulgar and ridiculous in the World State. The conversations between Helmholtz and John illustrate that even the most reflective and intelligent World State member is defined by the culture in which he has been raised.

MUSTAPHA MOND

Mustapha Mond is the most powerful and intelligent proponent of the World State. Early in the novel, it is his voice that explains the history of the World State and the philosophy upon which it is based. Later in the novel it is his debate with John that lays out the fundamental difference in values between World State society and the kind of society represented in Shakespeare's plays.

Mustapha Mond is a paradoxical figure. He reads Shakespeare and the Bible and he used to be an independent-minded scientist, but he also censors new ideas and controls a totalitarian state. For Mond, humankind's ultimate goals are stability and happiness, as opposed to emotions, human relations, and individual expression. By combining a firm commitment to the values of the World State with a nuanced understanding of its history and function, Mustapha Mond presents a formidable opponent for John, Bernard, and Helmholtz.

THEMES, MOTIFS & SYMBOLS

THEMES

Themes are the fundamental and often universal ideas explored in a literary work.

THE USE OF TECHNOLOGY TO CONTROL SOCIETY

Brave New World warns of the dangers of giving the state control over new and powerful technologies. One illustration of this theme is the rigid control of reproduction through technological and medical intervention, including the surgical removal of ovaries, the Bokanovsky Process, and hypnopaedic conditioning. Another is the creation of complicated entertainment machines that generate both harmless leisure and the high levels of consumption and production that are the basis of the World State's stability. *Soma* is a third example of the kind of medical, biological, and psychological technologies that *Brave New World* criticizes most sharply.

It is important to recognize the distinction between science and technology. Whereas the State talks about progress and science, what it really means is the bettering of technology, not increased scientific exploration and experimentation. The state uses science as a means to build technology that can create a seamless, happy, superficial world through things such as the "feelies." The state censors and limits science, however, since it sees the fundamental basis behind science, the search for truth, as threatening to the State's control. The State's focus on happiness and stability means that it uses the results of scientific research, inasmuch as they contribute to technologies of control, but does not support science itself.

THE CONSUMER SOCIETY

It is important to understand that *Brave New World* is not simply a warning about what *could* happen to society if things go wrong, it is also a satire of the society in which Huxley existed, and which still exists today. While the attitudes and behaviors of World State citizens at first appear bizarre, cruel, or scandalous, many clues point to the conclusion that the World State is simply an extreme—but logically developed—version of our society's economic values, in which individual happiness is defined as the ability to satisfy needs, and success as a society is equated with economic growth and prosperity.

THE INCOMPATIBILITY OF HAPPINESS AND TRUTH

Brave New World is full of characters who do everything they can to avoid facing the truth about their own situations. The almost universal use of the drug *soma* is probably the most pervasive example of such willful self-delusion. *Soma* clouds the realities of the present and replaces them with happy hallucinations, and is thus a tool for promoting social stability. But even Shakespeare can be used to avoid facing the truth, as John demonstrates by his insistence on viewing Lenina through the lens of Shakespeare's world, first as a Juliet and later as an "impudent strumpet." According to Mustapha Mond, the World State prioritizes happiness at the expense of truth by design: he believes that people are better off with happiness than with truth.

What are these two abstract entities that Mond juxtaposes? It seems clear enough from Mond's argument that happiness refers to the immediate gratification of every citizen's desire for food, sex, drugs, nice clothes, and other consumer items. It is less clear what Mond means by truth, or specifically *what* truths he sees the World State society as covering up. From Mond's discussion with John, it is possible to identify two main types of truth that the World State seeks to eliminate. First, as Mond's own past indicates, the World State controls and muffles all efforts by citizens to gain any sort of scientific, or empirical truth. Second, the government attempts to destroy all kinds of "human" truths, such as love, friendship, and personal connection. These two types of truth are quite different from each other: objective truth involves coming to a definitive conclusion of fact, while a "human" truth can only be explored, not defined. Yet both kinds of truth are united in the passion that an individual might feel for them. As a young man, Mustapha Mond became enraptured with the delight of making discoveries, just as John loves the language and intensity of Shakespeare. The search for truth then, also seems to involve a great deal of individual effort, of striving and fighting against odds. The very will to search for truth is an individual desire that the communal society of *Brave New World,* based as it is on anonymity and lack of thought, cannot allow to exist. Truth and individuality thus become entwined in the novel's thematic structure.

THE DANGERS OF AN ALL-POWERFUL STATE

Like George Orwell's *1984*, this novel depicts a dystopia in which an all-powerful state controls the behaviors and actions of its people in order to preserve its own stability and power. But a major difference between the two is that, whereas in *1984* control is maintained by constant government surveillance, secret police, and torture, power in *Brave New World* is maintained through technological interventions that start before birth and last until death, and that actually change what people want. The government of *1984* maintains power through force and intimidation. The government of *Brave New World* retains control by making its citizens so happy and superficially fulfilled that they don't care about their personal freedom. In *Brave New World* the consequences of state control are a loss of dignity, morals, values, and emotions—in short, a loss of humanity.

MOTIFS

Motifs are recurring structures, contrasts, or literary devices that can help to develop and inform the text's major themes.

"PNEUMATIC"

The word "pneumatic" is used with remarkable frequency to describe two things: Lenina's body and chairs. "Pneumatic" is an adjective that usually means that something has air pockets or works by means of compressed air. In the case of the chairs (in the feely theater and in Mond's office), it probably means that the chairs' cushions are inflated with air. In Lenina's case, the word is used by both Henry Foster and Benito Hoover to describe what she's like to have sex with. She herself remarks that her lovers usually find her "pneumatic," patting her legs as she does so. In reference to Lenina it means well-rounded, balloon-like, or bouncy, in reference to her flesh, and in particular her bosom. Huxley is not the only writer to use the word pneumatic in this sense, although it is an unusual usage. The use of this odd word to describe the physical characteristics of both a woman and a piece of furniture underscores the novel's theme that human sexuality has been degraded to the level of a commodity.

FORD, "MY FORD," "YEAR OF OUR FORD," ETC.

Throughout *Brave New World*, the citizens of the World State substitute the name of Henry Ford, the early twentieth-century industrialist and founder of the Ford Motor Company, wherever people in our own world would say Lord" (i.e., Christ). This demonstrates that even at the level of casual conversation and habit, religion has been replaced by reverence for technology—specifically the efficient, mechanized factory production of goods that Henry Ford pioneered.

ALIENATION

The motif of alienation provides a counterpoint to the motif of total conformity that pervades the World State. Bernard Marx, Helmholtz Watson, and John are alienated from the World State, each for his own reasons. Bernard is alienated because he is a misfit, too small and powerless for the position he has been conditioned to enjoy. Helmholtz is alienated for the opposite reason: he is too intelligent even to play the role of an Alpha Plus. John is alienated on multiple levels and at multiple sites: not only does the Indian community reject him, but he is both unwilling and unable to become part of the World State. The motif of alienation is one of the driving forces of the narrative: it provides the main characters with their primary motivations.

SEX

Brave New World abounds with references to sex. At the heart of the World State's control of its population is its rigid control over sexual mores and reproductive rights. Reproductive rights are controlled through an authoritarian system that sterilizes about two thirds of women, requires the rest to use contraceptives, and surgically removes ovaries when it needs to produce new humans. The act of sex is controlled by a system of social rewards for promiscuity and lack of commitment. John, an outsider, is tortured by his desire for Lenina and her inability to return his love as such. The conflict between John's desire for love and Lenina's desire for sex illustrates the profound difference in values between the World State and the humanity represented by Shakespeare's works.

SHAKESPEARE

Shakespeare provides the language through which John understands the world. Through John's use of Shakespeare, the novel makes contact with the rich themes explored in plays like *The Tempest*. It also creates a stark contrast between the utilitarian simplicity and inane babble of the World State's propaganda and the nuanced, elegant verse of a time "before Ford." Shakespeare's plays provide many examples of precisely the kind of human relations—passionate, intense, and often tragic—that the World State is committed to eliminating.

Symbols

Symbols are objects, characters, figures, or colors used to represent abstract ideas or concepts.

Soma

The drug *soma* is a symbol of the use of instant gratification to control the World State's populace. It is also a symbol of the powerful influence of science and technology on society. As a kind of "sacrament," it also represents the use of religion to control society.

SUMMARY & ANALYSIS

CHAPTER 1

SUMMARY: CHAPTER 1

The novel opens in the Central London Hatchery and Conditioning Centre. The year is A.F. 632 (632 years "after Ford"). The Director of Hatcheries and Conditioning is giving a group of students a tour of a factory that produces human beings and conditions them for their predestined roles in the World State. He explains to the boys that human beings no longer produce living offspring. Instead, surgically removed ovaries produce ova that are fertilized in artificial receptacles and incubated in specially designed bottles.

The Hatchery destines each fetus for a particular caste in the World State. The five castes are Alpha, Beta, Gamma, Delta, and Epsilon. Gamma, Delta, and Epsilon undergo the Bokanovsky Process which involves shocking an egg so that it divides to form up to ninety-six identical embryos, which then develop into ninety-six identical human beings. The Alpha and Beta embryos never undergo this dividing process, which can weaken the embryos. The Director explains that the Bokanovsky Process facilitates social stability because the clones it produces are predestined to perform identical tasks at identical machines. The cloning process is one of the tools the World State uses to implement its guiding motto: "Community, Identity, Stability."

The Director goes on to describe Podsnap's Technique which speeds up the ripening process of eggs within a single ovary. With this method, hundreds of related individuals can be produced from the ova and sperm of the same man and woman within two years. The average production rate using Podsnap's Technique is 11,000 brothers and sisters in 150 batches of identical twins. Called over by the director, Mr. Henry Foster, an employee at the plant, tells the attentive students that the record for this particular factory is over 16,000 siblings.

The Director and Henry Foster continue to explain the processes of the plant to the boys. After fertilization, the embryos travel on a conveyor belt in their bottles for 267 days, the gestation time period for a human fetus. On the last day, they are "decanted," or born. The entire process is designed to mimic the conditions within a human womb, including shaking every few meters to familiarize the fetuses with movement. Seventy percent of the female fetuses are sterilized; they are known as "freemartins." The fetuses undergo different treatments depending on their castes. Oxygen deprivation and alcohol treatment ensure the lower intelligence and smaller size of members of the three lower castes. Fetuses destined for work in the tropical climate are heat conditioned as embryos; during childhood, they undergo further conditioning to produce adults that are emotionally and physically suited to hot climates. The artificial process, says the Director, aims to make individuals accept and even like "their inescapable social destiny."

The Director and Henry Foster then introduce Lenina Crowne to the students. She explains that her job is to immunize the fetuses destined for the tropics with vaccinations for typhoid and sleeping sickness. In front of the boys, Henry reminds Lenina of their date for that afternoon, which the Director finds "charming." Henry goes on to explain that future rocket-plane engineers are conditioned to live in constant motion, and future chemical workers are conditioned to tolerate toxic chemicals. Henry wants to show the students the conditioning of Alpha Plus Intellectual fetuses, but the Director, looking at his watch, announces that the time is ten to three. He decides there is not enough time to see the Alpha Plus conditioning; he wants to make sure the students get to the Nurseries before the children there have awakened from their naps.

ANALYSIS: CHAPTER 1

Huxley's *Brave New World* can be seen as a critique of the overenthusiastic embrace of new scientific discoveries. The first chapter reads like a list of stunning scientific achievements: human cloning, rapid maturation, and prenatal conditioning. However, the satirical tone of the chapter makes it clear that this technology-based society is not a utopia, but the exact opposite. Like George Orwell's *1984*, *Brave New World* depicts a dystopia: a world of anonymous and dehumanized people dominated by a government made overwhelmingly powerful by the use of technology.

The almost religious regard in which the World State holds technology is apparent from the start. The starting date for the calendar is Henry Ford's introduction of the Model T, an automobile cheaply and efficiently produced by the assembly line system. All dates are preceded by "A.F.," "After Ford," just as today's calendar system begins with the birth of Jesus, A.D. (*Anno Domini*, meaning "in the year of the lord"). Other satirical hints of a warped religion are scattered throughout the text. The Predestinators, for example, are a farcical secular manifestation of the Calvinist religious belief that God predestines individuals for heaven or hell before birth. The World State's religious adherence to technology is far from innocent. In fact it becomes one of the pillars of stability for the totalitarian World State. As the Director says, "social stability" is the highest social goal, and through predestination and rigorous conditioning, individuals accept their given roles in society without question. The caste structure is created and maintained using specific tools, and it is technology that allows the most powerful members of the World State's ruling Alpha caste to solidify and justify the unequal distribution of power and status.

Conditioning individuals genetically, physically, and psychologically for their "inescapable social destinies" stabilizes the caste system by creating servants who love and fully accept their servility. Moreover, conditioning makes them virtually incapable of performing any other function than that to which they are assigned. The satirical tone of the text makes it clear that, though social stability may sound like an admirable goal, it can be used for the wrong reasons toward the wrong ends.

One theme emphasized repeatedly in this first chapter is the similarity between the production of humans in the Hatchery and the production of consumer goods on an assembly line. Everything about human reproduction is technologically managed to maximize efficiency and profit. Following the rule of supply and demand, the Predestinators project how many members of each caste will be needed, and the Hatchery produces human beings according to those figures. One of the keys of mass production is that every part is identical and interchangeable; a steering wheel from one Model T fits neatly onto the steering column of any other Ford. Similarly, in the Hatchery, human beings are standardized by the production of thousands of brothers and sisters in multiple groups of identical twins using the Bokanovsky and Podsnap Processes.

The lower castes are more subject to these forces of anonymity and mechanization. Members of the higher castes are decanted one by one, without any artificial intervention. Thus the higher castes retain at least some level of the individuality and creativity that is denied completely to the lower castes.

CHAPTER 2

SUMMARY: CHAPTER 2

The Director leads the group of students to the Nurseries. Posted on a notice board are the phrases, "Infant Nurseries. Neo-Pavlovian Conditioning Rooms." The students observe a Bokanovsky group of eight-month-old babies wearing the Delta caste's khaki-colored clothes. Some nurses present the babies with books and flowers. As the babies crawl toward the books and the flowers, cooing with pleasure, alarms ring shrilly. Then, the babies suffer a mild electric shock. Afterward, when the nurses offer the flowers and books to the babies, they shrink away and wail with terror.

The Director explains that after 200 repetitions of the same process, the children will have an instinctive hatred of books and flowers. A hatred for books is ingrained in the lower castes to prevent them from wasting the community's time reading books that might "decondition" them. The motivation for instilling a hatred for flowers is more complicated. The Director explains that Gammas, Deltas, and Epsilons were once conditioned to like flowers and nature in general. The idea was to compel them to visit the country often and "consume transport" in the process. But since nature is free, they consumed nothing other than transportation.

In order to increase the consumption of goods, The World State decided to abolish the love of nature while preserving the desire to use transportation. The lower castes are now conditioned to hate the countryside but to love country sports. All country sports in the World State require the use of elaborate apparatus. As a result, the lower castes now pay for both transportation and manufactured goods when they travel to the country for sporting events.

The Director begins to tell a story about a child named Reuben who has Polish-speaking parents. The students blush at the mere mention of the word "parent." References to sexual reproduction, including words like "mother" and "father," are now considered pornographic. In the World State, people only use such words in clinical discussions.

The Director continues with his story. One night, Reuben's parents left the radio on while he slept. The child woke up reciting a broadcast of a George Bernard Shaw speech verbatim. The parents did not understand English, so they thought something was wrong. Their doctor understood English and notified the medical press of the event. Reuben's overnight learning led to the discovery of sleep teaching, or hypnopaedia. The Director informs the students that the discovery of hypnopaedia came only twenty-three years after the first Ford Model T was sold. He makes the sign of the T on his stomach (as an observant Catholic might make the sign of the cross) and the students follow suit. He explains that researchers of hypnopaedia soon discovered that it was useless for intellectual training. Reuben could repeat the speech word for word, but had no idea what it meant. The place where hypnopaedia can be used, however, is moral training.

The Director leads the tour to a dormitory where some Beta children are sleeping. The Nurse informs them that the Elementary Sex lesson is over and the Elementary Class Consciousness lesson has just begun. A recorded voice whispers to each sleeping child. It states that Alpha children have to work harder than the other classes and it disparages the lower intelligence and inferiority of the lower castes. The voice teaches pride and happiness in the Beta caste: Betas do not have to work as hard as the cleverer Alphas, it explains, but they are still smarter than the Gammas, Deltas, and Epsilons. The Director explains that the lesson will be repeated one hundred and twenty times, three times a week, for thirty months. Hypnopaedia instills the fine distinctions and prejudices for which electric shocks and alarms are too crude. Hypnopaedia, the Director concludes, is "the greatest moralizing and socializing force of all time."

ANALYSIS: CHAPTER 2

The first half of the students' tour, described in the previous section, illustrates the World State's abuse of biological science in conditioning its citizens. This section focuses on the use of psychological technologies to control the future behavior of World State citizens. Conditioning, combined with prenatal treatment, creates individuals without individuality: each one is programmed to behave exactly like the next. This system allows for social stability, economic productivity within narrow constraints, and a society dominated by unthinking obedience and infantile behavior.

The conditioning technique used to instill a dislike for flowers and books in infants is modeled after the research of Ivan Pavlov, a Russian scientist. Pavlov demonstrated that dogs could be trained to salivate at the ringing of a bell if the sound was consistently visually associated with food. This led to the observation that other kinds of responses could also be conditioned. His work became known to Western science in the decade before *Brave New World* was written.

By applying Pavlovian theory to human infants, the state literally programs human beings to uphold the status quo.

The conditioning also drives the population to support the capitalist economic system. Because the World State wants children to be loyal consumers as adults, the importance of the individual is diminished in order to further the interests of the larger community. Even during their off-work hours, World State citizens serve the interests of production and, therefore, the interests of the whole economy and society, by consuming transportation and expensive sporting equipment. Any opportunity for individual, idiosyncratic behavior that might not feed the economy is eliminated.

CHAPTER 3

Mother, monogamy, romance.

(See QUOTATIONS, p. 57)

SUMMARY: CHAPTER 3

The Director leads the students to the garden, where several hundred naked children are playing. The Director remarks that "in Our Ford's day," games involved no more than a ball or two, a few sticks, and maybe a net. Such simple apparatus did nothing to increase consumption. In the current World State, all games, like "Centrifugal Bumble-puppy," involve complicated machines.

The Director is interrupted by the cries of a little boy sitting in the bushes. It soon becomes clear that the little boy, for some reason, is uncomfortable with the erotic play in which the children are encouraged to participate. After the boy is whisked off to see the psychologist, the Director astounds the students by explaining that sexual play during childhood and adolescence used to be considered abnormal and immoral. When he begins to explain the deleterious effects of sexual repression, a man interrupts him. The Director reverently introduces the man as "his fordship" Mustapha Mond. At the complex, four thousand electric clocks simultaneously strike four, marking the shift change. Henry Foster and Lenina each head up to the changing rooms in preparation for their date. While heading to the rooms, Henry snubs Bernard Marx who is said to have an unsavory reputation.

The narrative suddenly begins to shift back and forth between three different scenes, splicing in Mustapha Mond's speech to the boys with scenes of Henry's conversation in the male changing room and Lenina's conversation in the female training room. This SparkNote will describe Mond's speech first, and then the two changing room conversations.

The students are overwhelmed by meeting Mond, the Resident Controller for Western Europe, and one of only ten World Controllers. Mond quotes Ford, saying, "History is bunk" (an actual quote from the real-life Henry Ford) in order to explain why the students have not learned any of the history that the Director explains to them. The Director glances at him nervously. He has heard rumors that Mond keeps forbidden books, such as Bibles and poetry collections, locked in a safe. Mond, aware of the Director's unease, condescendingly reassures him that he does not plan to corrupt the students.

Mond begins to describe life in the time before the World State began its policy of tight control over reproduction, child-rearing, and social relations. He likens the narrow channeling of emotion and desire to water under pressure in a pipe. One hole produces a strong jet. However, many small holes produce calm streams of water. Strong emotion, inspired by family relationships, sexual repression, and delayed satisfaction of desire, goes directly against stability. Without stability, civilization cannot exist. Before the existence of the World State, the instability caused by strong emotions led to disease, war, and social unrest that resulted in millions of deaths and untold suffering and misery.

Mond describes the initial resistance to the World State's use of hypnopaedia, the caste system, and artificial gestation. But after the Nine Years' War, which involved horrible chemical and biological warfare, an intense propaganda campaign, including the suppression of all books published before A.F. 150, began to weaken the resistance. Religion, Shakespeare, museums, and families all passed into obscurity. The date of the introduction of the Model T was chosen as the start of the new era, and all crosses had their tops cut off to make them into Ts. Six years of pharmaceutical research yielded *soma*, the perfect drug. The problem of old age was solved, and people could now retain the mental and physical character of youth throughout life. No one was allowed to sit alone and think. No one was allowed "leisure from pleasure."

In the changing room at the end of the workday, Bernard overhears Henry talking with the Assistant Predestinator about Lenina. The Predestinator suggests a "feely" (a movie involving senses of touch and smell) that Henry might want to attend. While discussing Lenina admiringly, Henry tells the Assistant that he should "have her" some time. The conversation disgusts Bernard. The Assistant notices his glum expression and he and Henry decide to bait him. Henry offers Bernard some *soma,* infuriating him. They laugh as Bernard curses them.

The scene shifts to a public bathroom and showering room, where Lenina is chatting with Fanny Crowne. At age nineteen, Fanny is starting to take a temporary Pregnancy Substitute because she feels "out of sorts." The Pregnancy Substitute mimics the hormonal effects of pregnancy. Fanny expresses surprise that Lenina is still dating Henry exclusively after four months. She advises Lenina to be more promiscuous, as a virtuous member of World State should. Lenina mentions that Bernard Marx, an Alpha Plus hypnopaedia specialist, invited her to the Savage Reservation. Fanny warns that Bernard has a bad reputation for spending time alone and is smaller and less confident than other Alphas. Fanny mentions the rumors that someone might have accidentally injected alcohol into his blood surrogate when he was in the bottle. Lenina decides to accept Bernard's invitation because she thinks Bernard is sweet and wants to see the Reservation. Fanny admires Lenina's Malthusian belt, a contraceptive holder that was a gift from Henry.

ANALYSIS: CHAPTER 3

As the Director and Mustapha Mond explain to the boys how the World State works in an abstract way, the interspliced scenes of Lenina and Bernard show the society in action. The sexual play of the children at recess, the boys' discomfort at the word "mother," Lenina's relaxed nakedness, and the conversation between Henry and the Predestinator all serve to illustrate how the traditional taboos regarding sexuality have been discarded. Bernard is the sole character to protest—almost silently—the way the system works. His discomfort with the commodification of sex marks him as a misfit. It is worth noting that the novel explicitly establishes that Bernard's dissatisfaction with the State stems from his own isolation within it, introducing Bernard with the words "Those who feel themselves despised do well to look despising." Bernard may be a rebel, but that rebellion does not come from any ideological objection to the World State. It comes from a sense that he might never fully belong to that society. This facet of Bernard's character will be brought into play as the novel progresses.

In addition to prenatal and postnatal conditioning, the World State controls the behavior of its members through the forces of social conformity and social criticism. Lenina's friend Fanny warns her that the Director does not like it when Hatchery workers fail to conform to the expected promiscuity standards. Even as an adult, a World State citizen must fear being seen doing something "shameful" or "abnormal." The adult citizen has no private life. As Lenina notes, the only thing that one does when one is alone in the World State is sleep, and one can't do that forever. In and out of the office, the adult citizen is under surveillance to ensure that his or her body and mind are following the World State's moral value system. Both peers and superiors, like Fanny and the Director, are constantly watching to ensure that each citizen is behaving appropriately.

In his long speech about the history of the World State, Mustapha Mond blames the previously sacred institutions of family, love, motherhood, and marriage for causing social instability in the old society. As Mond explains it, these old institutions shared the work of mediating the conflict between the individual's interests and the interests of society with the State, but the personal institutions and State institutions were themselves out of alignment, creating instability. Individuals cannot always be relied upon to choose the path of most stability since family, love, and marriage produce divided allegiances. Freely acting individuals must constantly weigh the moral value and the moral consequences of their actions. Mond argues that the divided allegiances of individuals produce social instability. For this reason, the World State has eliminated all traces of non-State institutions. The citizen is socialized to only have an allegiance to the State; personal connections of all sorts are discouraged, and even the desire to develop such connections is conditioned away. The constant availability of physical satisfaction evident in the feelies, the abundance of *soma*, the easy attainment of sex through state sanctioned promiscuity, and the lack of any historical knowledge that might point to an alternate way of life, ensure that the way of life developed and instituted by the World State will not be threatened.

Mustapha Mond and the Director spend a good deal of time discussing the importance of consumption. They are really talking about creating a population that will always want more—a captive market created by conditioning that will want whatever goods the World State produces. This culture of constant consumption allows the Government to act as a supplier, propelling the economy and creating a happy community dependent on its supplier. But the economic discussion led by Mond and the Director does not refer only to the economy of money and goods. In *Brave New World*, everything, including sex, operates according to the logic of supply and demand. Citizens are taught to view one another, and themselves, as commodities to be consumed like any other manufactured good. Bernard rebels against this sentiment when he notes that Henry and the Predestinator view Lenina as a "piece of meat"—and that Lenina thinks of herself the same way. Consumption as a way of life is never justified by the World State; it is taken as a way of life.

In Mustapha Mond's discussion of history, *Brave New World* gives some thought to a theme that George Orwell explores in detail in *1984*. Implicit in Mond's statement that "history is bunk" and his discussion of the history of the World State, is the fact that Mond and the other nine World Controllers have a monopoly on historical knowledge. This ensures their positions of power. In *1984*, Orwell describes the mechanisms of this manipulation, as the government of Oceania actively revises history in order to serve its political goals from moment to moment. But in the World State, active revision is unnecessary because the population is conditioned to believe that, as Mond says, "history is bunk." Because they are trained to see history as worthless, they are trapped in the present, unable to imagine alternative ways of life. It is unclear why Mond takes the time to explain the history of the World State to the boys, though it certainly is a convenient way of explaining a possible pathway from the reader's world to that of the World State.

CHAPTERS 4–6

SUMMARY: CHAPTER 4

When Lenina tells Bernard in front of a big group of coworkers that she accepts his invitation to see the Savage Reservation, Bernard reacts with embarrassment. His suggestion that they discuss it privately confuses Lenina. She saunters off to meet Henry. Bernard feels terrible because Lenina behaved like a "healthy and virtuous English girl"— that is, someone unafraid of discussing her sexual life in public. When the genial Benito Hoover strikes up a conversation, Bernard rushes away. Lenina and Henry fly off on their date in Henry's helicopter, and look down upon their world in perfect contentment.

Ordering a pair of Delta-Minus attendants to get his helicopter ready for flight, Bernard betrays his insecurity about his size. The lower castes associate larger size with higher status, so he has trouble getting them to follow his orders. Bernard contemplates his feelings of alienation and becomes irritable. He visits his friend, Helmholtz Watson, a lecturer at the College of Emotional Engineering. Helmholtz is an extremely intelligent, attractive, and properly sized Alpha Plus who works in propaganda. Some of Helmholtz's superiors think he is a little too smart for his own good. The narrator agrees with them, noting that "a mental excess had produced in Helmholtz Watson effects very similar to those which, in Bernard Marx, were the result of a physical defect." The friendship between Bernard and Helmholtz springs from their mutual dissatisfaction with the status quo and their shared inclination to view themselves as individuals. Once together, Bernard boasts that Lenina has accepted his invitation, but Helmholtz shows little interest. Helmholtz is preoccupied with the thought that his writing talent could be better used than simply for writing hypnopaedic phrases. His work leaves him feeling empty and unfulfilled. Bernard becomes nervous, jumping up at one point because he thinks, wrongly, that someone is listening at the door.

SUMMARY: CHAPTER 5

After a game of Obstacle Golf, Henry and Lenina fly in a helicopter over a crematorium where phosphorous is collected from burning bodies for fertilizer. They drink coffee with *soma* before heading off to the Westminster Abbey Cabaret. They take another *soma* dose before they return to Henry's apartment. Although the repeated doses of *soma* have made them almost completely oblivious to the world around them, Lenina remembers to use her contraceptives.

> *Orgy-porgy, Ford and fun,*
> *Kiss the girls and make them One.*
> *Boys at one with girls at peace;*
> *Orgy-porgy gives release.*
>
> *(See* QUOTATIONS, *p. 58)*

Every other Thursday, Bernard has to take part in Solidarity Service at the Fordson Community Singery. The participants sit twelve to a table, alternating men and women. While a rousing hymn plays, the participants pass a cup of strawberry ice cream *soma* and take a *soma* tablet with it. They work themselves into a frenzy of exultation and the ceremony ends in a sex orgy that leaves Bernard feeling more isolated than ever.

SUMMARY: CHAPTER 6

Lenina convinces Bernard to attend a wrestling match. He behaves gloomily the entire afternoon and, despite Lenina's urging, refuses to take *soma*. During the return trip, he stops his helicopter and hovers over the Channel. She begs him to take her away from the rushing emptiness of the water after he tells her that the silence makes him feel like an individual. Eventually he takes a large dose of *soma*, and has sex with her.

The next day, Bernard tells Lenina that he did not really want to have sex with her the first night; he would have preferred to act like an adult instead. Then he goes to get the Director's permission to visit the Reservation. He braces himself for the Director's disapproval of his unusual behavior. When the Director presents the permit, he mentions that he took a trip there with a woman twenty years before. She was lost during a storm and has not been seen since. When Bernard says that he must have suffered a terrible shock, the Director immediately realizes that he has been revealing too much of his personal life. He criticizes Bernard for his antisocial behavior and threatens to exile him to Iceland if his impropriety persists. Bernard leaves the office feeling proud of being considered a rebel.

> *A gramme in time saves nine . . . One cubic centimetre cures ten gloomy sentiments . . . Everybody's happy nowadays . . .*
>
> *(See* QUOTATIONS, *p. 59)*

Lenina and Bernard travel to the Reservation. When they present themselves to the Warden to get his signature on the permit, he launches into a long series of facts about the place. Bernard suddenly remembers that he left the scent tap on at his apartment, an oversight that could end up being extremely expensive. He endures the Warden's seemingly endless speech and then hurries to phone Helmholtz to ask him to turn off the tap for him. Helmholtz has bad news: he tells Bernard that the Director is planning to carry out his threat of exiling him to Iceland. Bernard is no longer proud and rebellious now that the Director's threat has become a reality. Instead, the news crushes and frightens him. Lenina persuades him to take *soma*.

ANALYSIS: CHAPTERS 4–6

Bernard's role as the protagonist—a role that John will later take over—continues in this section. Increasingly, he appears less like a political rebel and more like a social misfit who believes that changing society is the only way for him to fit in. His conversations with Helmholtz reveal that he is boastful of his liaison with Lenina, afraid of being caught criticizing the World State, and subservient to Helmholtz when it comes to matters of real rebellion. Bernard is a paradoxical character, at one moment lusting after Lenina and at the next hoping that he will have the strength to resist her advances.

Helmholtz, whom we meet for the first time in this section, has the exact opposite of Bernard's problem. Whereas Bernard is too small and strange for his caste, Helmholtz is, if anything, too perfect. His success with women, in his career, and in every other aspect of his life has led him to believe that there must be something more to life than high-tech sports, easy sex, and repetitive slogans. He talks to Bernard because Bernard shares his dislike for the system, but he is aware that Bernard's dislike has a different basis than his own.

The setting of these chapters changes rapidly: from the workplace to Helmholtz's apartment; from Henry's helicopter to Westminster Abbey Cabaret to a Crematorium; from Bernard's apartment to the Community Singery; and so on. Some of the scene-shifting is simply used to flesh out a day in the life of a World State member. Lenina and Henry's visit to the Westminster Abbey Cabaret is a blunt joke about the uses to which the World State puts ancient religious sites.

> *Every one works for every one else. We can't do without any one. Even Epsilons are useful. We couldn't do without Epsilons.*
>
> (See QUOTATIONS, *p. 58*)

As Henry and Lenina contemplate the crematorium, they come close to acknowledging that the caste system may be less than perfect. But then Lenina, troubled and disliking, retreats to one of her stock hypnopaedic phrases, regains her happiness, and the crisis is over. Once again, she is happy to be in her caste and disdainful of those in other castes. This episode, made possible by the setting of a helicopter trip past a Crematorium, shows how conditioning can keep the population from questioning the assumptions of the state in which they live. The biggest change in setting is from the World State to the Reservation, though a detailed description of the Reservation is held until the next section.

Although the World State most obviously controls its members by conditioning them and gratifying their desires, there are hints that stability is maintained through methods that are still more sinister. Bernard's sudden fear that someone is listening to his heretical conversation with Helmholtz suggests a totalitarian aspect of the World State. Outside work hours, World State citizens attend strictly regulated, scheduled social activities and never spend any time alone. The lack of time for reflection keeps them occupied and docile. Bernard's fear shows that he is aware of the unwritten but potentially serious consequences of his heretical beliefs.

CHAPTERS 7–8

SUMMARY: CHAPTER 7

At the Reservation, Lenina watches a community celebration. The pounding of the drums reminds her of Solidarity Services and Ford's Day celebrations. The images of an eagle and a man on a cross are raised, and a youth walks into the center of a pile of writhing snakes. A man whips him, drawing blood until the youth collapses. Lenina is horrified.

John, a handsome blond youth in Indian dress, surprises Lenina and Bernard by speaking perfect English. He says that he wanted to be the sacrifice, but the town would not let him. He explains that his mother, Linda, came from the Other Place outside the Reservation. During a visit to the Reservation, she fell and suffered an injury, but was rescued by some Indians who found her and brought her to the village, where she has lived ever since. His father, also from the Other Place, was named Tomakin. Bernard realizes that "Tomakin" is actually Thomas, the Director, but says nothing for the moment.

John introduces Lenina and Bernard to his mother, Linda. Wrinkled, overweight, and missing teeth, she disgusts Lenina. Linda explains that John was born because something went wrong with her contraceptives. She could not get an abortion on the Reservation and felt too ashamed to go back to the World State with a baby. Linda explains that, after starting her new life in the Indian village, she followed all her conditioning and slept with any man she pleased, but some women beat her for taking their men to bed.

SUMMARY: CHAPTER 8

John tells Bernard that he grew up listening to Linda's fabulous stories about the Other Place. But he also felt isolated and rejected, partly because his mother slept with so many men and partly because the people of the village never accepted him. Linda took a lover, Popé, who brought her an alcoholic drink called mescal. She began drinking heavily. Meanwhile, despite being forbidden from taking part in the Indian's rituals, John absorbed the culture around him. Linda taught him to read, at first by drawing on the wall and later using a guide for Beta Embryo-Store Workers that she had happened to bring with her. He asked her questions about the World State, but she could tell him very little about how it worked. One day, Popé brought the complete works of Shakespeare to Linda's house. John read it avidly until he could quote passages by heart. The plays gave voice to all of his repressed emotions.

Bernard asks John if he would like to go to London with him. He has an ulterior motive that he keeps to himself: he wants to embarrass the Director by exposing him as John's father. John accepts the proposal, but insists that Linda be allowed to go with him. Bernard promises to seek permission to take both of them. John quotes a line from *The Tempest* to express his feelings of joy at finally getting to see the Other World that he had heard about as a child: "O brave new world that has such people in it." Blushing, he asks if Bernard is married to Lenina. Bernard laughs and tells him that he certainly is not. He also cautions John to wait until he sees the World State before he becomes enraptured with it.

ANALYSIS: CHAPTERS 7–8

These chapters contain a crucial plot development: the meeting of Bernard and John. John is an outcast who has always dreamed of living in the World State; Bernard is a World State misfit who is looking for some way to fit in. Their meeting sets in motion a chain of events that produces shattering consequences for both of them.

Huxley uses a literary device called a flashback to bring Bernard, and the reader, up to date on John's background. This device allows Huxley to present a collage of images from John's childhood that would otherwise fit awkwardly into the overall structure of the narrative. If the narrative had been presented in strict chronological order, John and Linda's story would have been told first. Coming in the middle of the novel, it has a greater impact because the reader already knows about the vast differences between World State and Reservation culture. Linda's failure to fit in on the Reservation, and John's confused upbringing, only make sense within the context that has already been provided.

Linda's experiences on the Reservation, as described by herself and by John, demonstrate the extent to which the World State citizens are dependent upon "civilization"—that is, on a life that is completely structured by the state. On the Reservation, she is practically helpless: she does not know how to mend clothing, cook, or clean, and the very idea of taking care of a child horrifies her. She turns to mescal as a poor substitute for *soma*, which until then had been her only method for dealing with unpleasant situations.

John is a cultural hybrid, absorbing both his mother's culture and that of the Indians on the Reservation. But he is also culturally adrift. The Reservation's community does not accept him, and Linda's Other Place is a distant world he only hears about in stories. So he turns to Shakespeare in his isolation and absorbs a third cultural value system.

Shakespeare's *The Tempest* provides an important parallel to *Brave New World,* and the two texts relate to one another on many levels. In the play, Prospero and his daughter Miranda are exiled to an island because Prospero's brother betrayed him in order to gain political power. The only inhabitant on the Island is a native, Caliban, to whose deceased mother the island had belonged. Prospero usurps control of the island and decides to raise Caliban as a slave because he pities him and intends to civilize him. Shakespeare deftly portrays Caliban as an angry, violent figure, who could easily be interpreted as less than human, ruled by bestial appetites rather than higher instincts. When a ship arrives on the island, two of the stewards introduce Caliban to liquor, and liquor becomes Caliban's "God." Yet Shakespeare also manages to imbue Caliban with all the complexities of the colonized individual. Caliban may be angry and violent, but he has been oppressed by Prospero. Caliban becomes enthralled by liquor and sees it as a god, but he has never seen alcohol before, and the effects of becoming drunk must be staggering to him. Prospero purports to help Caliban by "civilizing" him, but Caliban resents Prospero for the theft of his home. Prospero views Caliban's resentment as unfounded and as evidence of his bestial nature, and this prompts him to treat Caliban even more harshly. Caliban responds with violent action that only increases Prospero's belief that Caliban is an animal. In *The Tempest,* Caliban is both "savage" and a "Noble Savage," he is utterly displaced in every community, just as John is on the Reservation, and will come to be in the World State.

Both *The Tempest* and *Brave New World* can be interpreted as allegories of colonization. Prospero decides to raise Caliban and "civilize" him in the same way that European colonials attempted to "civilize" the African, Asian, and native American cultures with which they came into contact. For British and other European colonizers, civilizing the savages was a process of replacing native cultures and languages with the culture and language of the colonizer. The colonizers effectively separated colonized peoples from their own history and culture, making it more difficult for the latter to rebel against the new implanted culture that had become their own. The entire World State is built on just such a premise, effacing the past and all its cultural legacies. The World State, in a sense, has colonized everyone.

CHAPTERS 9–10

SUMMARY: CHAPTER 9

Lenina, disgusted by the Reservation, takes enough *soma* to inca-
pacitate herself for eighteen hours. Bernard flies to Santa Fé to call
Mustapha Mond. He repeats his story to a succession of secretaries
before finally reaching the World Controller. Mond agrees that John
and Linda are a matter of scientific interest to the World State. He
instructs Bernard to visit the Warden of the Reservation to pick up
the orders that will release John and Linda into his care. Meanwhile,
fearful that Bernard and Lenina have left without him, John breaks
into the cabin where Lenina is still on *soma*-holiday. He rifles
through her things before he finds her passed out on the bed. He
gazes at her, quietly quoting passages from *Romeo and Juliet*. He
wants to touch her but fears that it would defile her. As he gazes at
her, Bernard's helicopter approaches, and John is able to run from
the house and hide his trespass.

SUMMARY: CHAPTER 10

Back at the Hatchery, the Director tells Henry that he plans to dismiss
Bernard in front of dozens of high-caste workers as a public example.
He explains that Bernard's unorthodox behavior threatens stability.
Sacrificing one individual for the greater good of the society is no great
loss since the Hatchery can churn out dozens of new babies.

When Bernard arrives, the Director declares Bernard "heretical"
because he refuses to behave like an infant and does not immediately
seek to gratify his own desires. He tells Bernard that he is being
transferred to Iceland. But then Bernard presents Linda and John.
Linda accuses the Director of making her have a baby and the room
suddenly falls silent. John falls at the Director's feet and cries, "My
father!" The workers break out into peals of hysterical laughter as
the Director rushes from the room.

ANALYSIS: CHAPTERS 9–10

In these chapters the interlude at the Reservation ends and John's
life in the World State begins. The conflict between John's values
and the social mores of the World State starts to become obvious.
The shift of setting, from the Reservation in New Mexico to the
World State in England, foreshadows the shift that is about to take
place in the lives of both John and Bernard.

John's character is revealed more fully in his confrontations with World State culture. His struggle to suppress his desire to touch Lenina demonstrates the moral code that he has internalized from Shakespeare and from the "savages" on the Reservation. A World State resident would have gone for instant gratification. John finds himself in the unenviable position of living in the World State without World State conditioning. He is attracted to Lenina, but his views on sex are so radically different from hers that conflict is inevitable. The struggle between John's intense desires and his equally intense self-control is a major facet of his character.

John's habit of quoting lines from Shakespeare's plays not only highlights his distance from World State society, it also serves as a reminder of the distance between our society, in which Shakespeare is revered as a writer with deep insight into human nature, and World State society, in which Shakespeare is unknown and even incomprehensible.

Stylistically, John's Shakespearean quotations contrast vividly with the utterances of the World State citizens. But there is one notable similarity between them. Both the World State citizens *and* John habitually speak in quotes and soundbites. Hypnopaedic messages like "A gramme in time saves nine," are on everybody's lips in the World State. At times the conversations between John and Lenina degenerate into a war of propaganda, each person spewing memorized phrases without even stopping to think about them. John's propaganda sounds more palatable than Lenina's, because Shakespeare's poetic lines put the hypnopaedic messages to shame. Next to Shakespeare, "progress is lovely" sounds cheap and trashy. The juxtaposition of the two contributes to the satirical tone of the novel.

The confrontation between Bernard and the Director illustrates the power of social condemnation. The Director decides to denounce Bernard in front of the other workers in order to make an example out of him. In part, World State members are forced to conform merely by peer pressure and the threat of public shame. Bernard turns the Director's ploy on its head by shaming him with the spectacle of John and Linda. Bernard's willingness to use John and Linda for his own gain further helps to portray him as someone who will do anything to gain social standing. By presenting Linda and John to the Director in front of the workers, he not only manages to save his own position but also to spitefully attack the Director and reduce his social standing.

Lenina's role throughout this chapter is a passive one, for the obvious reason that she is on *soma*-holiday for most of it. Going on *soma*-holiday is her only way of dealing with the negative emotions aroused by the Reservation. It is particularly ironic that she goes on *soma*-holiday in the middle of what should have been a real holiday (her vacation).

CHAPTERS 11–12

SUMMARY: CHAPTER 11

The Director resigns in disgrace, and Bernard is able to keep his job. John, known as "the Savage," becomes an instant society hit. Linda takes *soma* continually and falls into a half-awake, half-asleep state of intoxication. Bernard experiences unprecedented popularity as John's appointed guardian. He boasts about his thriving sex life to Helmholtz, but Helmholtz responds only with a gloomy silence that offends Bernard. Bernard decides to stop speaking to him. He shamelessly parades his unorthodox behavior, thinking that his popularity as the Savage's discoverer and guardian will protect him. He writes Mond to tell him that John finds "civilized infantility" too easy. Bernard says he agrees with John's verdict. Mond, reading the heretical letter, thinks he might have to teach Bernard a lesson.

The sight of dozens of identical twins in a factory sickens John. With bitter irony, he echoes Shakespeare's line, "O brave new world that has such people in it." He refuses to take *soma* and visits his mother often. He visits Eton where Alpha children laugh at a film of "savages" beating themselves with whips on a Reservation.

Lenina likes John but cannot tell if he likes her. She takes him to a "feely," entitled *Three Weeks in a Helicopter,* that tells the story of a black man who kidnaps a blond Beta-Plus woman for his own enjoyment. John hates the movie, but it reinvigorates his passion for Lenina. His shame at his physical desire overwhelms him. To Lenina's bewilderment, John refuses to have sex with her. He locks himself in his room and reads Shakespeare's *Othello.* Lenina returns to her room and takes *soma.*

SUMMARY: CHAPTER 12

Bernard arranges a large party of important people, promising them a chance to meet "the Savage." But when they arrive, John refuses to leave his room. Bernard is humiliated and embarrassed as all of his guests, including the Arch-Community-Songster of Canterbury, leave in contempt. Lenina is disappointed that she cannot see John again to find out why he behaved so strangely after the feely. The Arch-Community-Songster warns Bernard that he should be more careful in his criticisms of the World State.

Bernard sinks back into his former melancholia now that his newfound success has evaporated. He makes John his scapegoat. Bernard is simultaneously grateful and resentful that Helmholtz gives him the friendship he needs without criticizing him for his earlier unfriendliness. Helmholtz has gotten himself into trouble for reading some unorthodox rhymes to his students at the college. But he is excited to have finally found a voice of his own.

John and Helmholtz meet, and take to one another right away. Bernard is jealous of their affection for one another and wishes he had never brought them together. He takes *soma* to escape his feelings. John reads passages from Shakespeare to Helmholtz. The poetry enraptures Helmholtz, but when John reads a passage from *Romeo and Juliet* about Juliet's parents trying to persuade her to marry Paris, Helmholtz bursts into laughter. The absurdity of having a mother and father is not the only thing that he finds funny; the fact that anyone would make a fuss over which man a girl should have is even funnier. John locks his book away because Helmholtz's laughter insults and wounds him.

ANALYSIS: CHAPTERS 11–12

In this section John gets a thorough introduction to World State society, which, for the most part, disgusts him. He perceives the culture of the World State to be superficial, inhumane, and immoral.

The relationship between John and Bernard dramatizes the major themes of *The Tempest*. John, who originally believed he would play the part of Miranda, learning to love the new world revealed to him, becomes known as "the Savage" and takes on a role similar to Caliban's; Bernard, by exposing John to civilization and expecting that to win John's everlasting gratitude, plays Prospero to John's Caliban.

The fate of John's mother, Linda, demonstrates what Mustaph Mond meant in suggesting that truth and happiness are incompatible. Everyone but John is content to allow Linda to abuse *soma*, even though they know it will kill her within a month or two. The doctor's explanation to John demonstrates the World State's callous attitude that human beings are things that should be "used up until they wear out." Just as with manufactured goods, when people get old and worn out, they become disposable. Linda goes on permanent *soma*-holiday, living out the short remainder of her life in a blissful haze of hallucinations and fantasies.

Bernard's personal reasons for allowing Linda to succumb to *soma* are even more unpleasant. Everyone in London clamors to see John, but they are equally determined not to see Linda. With Linda safely out of the way, Bernard is free to use John for his own purposes. Through his exploitation of John, Bernard demonstrates that his previous dissatisfaction with the World State had merely stemmed from his desire to enjoy more of its privileges, rather than from any true desire to live as an "adult" (which is how he had presented the matter to Lenina on their first date). When he becomes successful and begins to enjoy the benefits of his Alpha status, he even drops his friendship with Helmholtz, a nonconformist with an increasingly bad reputation. Helmholtz threatens Bernard's newfound success.

The feely that John attends with Lenina involves some old racist stereotypes, but it is quite complicated in its irony. It begins with a scene in which a "gigantic negro" copulates with a blonde woman. This scene in itself would be highly shocking and taboo to Huxley's white, middle-class, early-twentieth-century audience, but so far the feely-goers find it perfectly conventional. They even marvel at the realistic special effects. What the audience within the book finds shocking is when the black man, following a blow to the head that erases his conditioning, kidnaps the blonde for a monogamous three-week sexscapade in a helicopter. It's shocking to them because of the monogamy. Finally, three Alpha males rescue her and order is restored.

This scene reminds the reader of a feature of movies that is even older than Huxley's novel. Theatergoers love to watch characters in movies transgress against the rules that the viewers themselves have to abide by. This vicarious enjoyment is given a thin veneer of respectability through a decorous ending that restores the status quo. But the fact remains that the audience enjoys fantasizing about the transgression. In part, this whole scene is Huxley's joke, but it is also possible that monogamy is not as unusual a fantasy in the World State as we have been led to believe.

The scene in which John reads *Romeo and Juliet* demonstrates the power of conditioning. Even though Helmholtz is fairly unorthodox, he is still a product of World State conditioning. He appreciates the artistic value of Shakespeare's language, but he does not appreciate the drama of Juliet's parents trying to convince her to marry Paris. Because John identifies his desire for Lenina with the love between *Romeo and Juliet,* Helmholtz's laughter insults both his cultural values and his own innermost feelings. But Helmholtz cannot help it; the situations and emotions expressed in the play mean something very different to him than they do to John.

CHAPTERS 13–15

SUMMARY: CHAPTER 13

Henry invites Lenina to a feely, but she declines. He notices that she is upset and suggests that she might need a "Violent Passion Surrogate," or V.P.S. Later she complains to Fanny that she still does not know what it is like to sleep with a savage. Fanny warns her that it is unseemly to become obsessed over one man, and that she should find someone else to take her mind off of him. Lenina replies that she wants only John. Other men simply cannot distract her.

Lenina takes *soma* and visits John, intending to seduce him. She remarks that he does not seem pleased to see her. John falls to his knees and begins quoting Shakespeare to express his adoration. He speaks about marriage and declares his love for her. She asks why he had not said anything if he had wanted her all along. However, his talk about lifelong commitments and growing old together horrifies her.

Lenina presses her body against his and begins to remove her clothes. John becomes furious and terrified. He calls her a whore and slaps her. She locks herself in the bathroom while John reenacts King Lear's disgusted tirade against womankind and biological generation (*King Lear*, IV.vi.120-127). The phone rings and he answers it. Lenina hears him leave the apartment.

SUMMARY: CHAPTER 14

John hurries to the Park Lane Hospital for the Dying. He whispers impatiently to a nurse that he wants to see his mother. Blushing furiously at his use of the word "mother," she leads him to Linda's bed. John sits next to her in tears, trying to remember the good times they had together. A troop of eight-year-old Bokanovsky boys gathers around Linda, asking why she is so fat and ugly. John angers the nurse when he strikes one particularly offensive child. She criticizes him for interfering with the children's death conditioning and leads them away.

Linda mistakes John for Popé. He shakes her angrily, demanding that she recognize him as her son. She says his name, starts to recite a hypnopaedic phrase from her childhood, and then begins to choke. He rushes to the nurse in a fit of grief to ask for help, but Linda is dead by the time they get to her ward. John sobs uncontrollably while the nurse worries about the damage done to the children's death-conditioning. She hands out chocolate éclairs to the Bokanovsky twins. One twin points to Linda's body and asks John, "Is she dead?" John pushes him to the floor and rushes out of the ward.

SUMMARY: CHAPTER 15

In the hospital vestibule, John encounters two Bokanovsky groups of Delta twins picking up their *soma* rations after their shift. With bitter irony he recalls the lines, "How many goodly creatures are there here! How beauteous mankind is! O brave new world." With "O brave new world" echoing in his head, John cries out for them to stop taking the *soma* rations. He tells them that it is a poison meant to enslave them and asks them to choose freedom. The man distributing the *soma* calls Bernard at home. Helmholtz answers the phone and relays the news about John's statements to Bernard. They rush to the hospital together.

The uncomprehending faces of the Delta workers infuriate John. He throws the *soma* rations out a window. The Deltas rush at him in fury. Helmholtz, who has just arrived, jumps into the fray to help defend John. Bernard hesitates. He knows John and Helmholtz might be killed if he doesn't help, but he is afraid of being killed while trying to help them. He feels shame at his indecision. The police arrive, spraying *soma* vapor and a powerful anesthetic. Meanwhile, a recorded voice asks why the rioters are not happy together. Before long, the Deltas are crying, kissing one another, and apologizing. Their *soma* rations are quickly restored. The police ask Helmholtz and John to come quietly. Bernard tries to slip out the door unobserved, but is caught before he can escape.

ANALYSIS: CHAPTERS 13–15

The dramatic riot incited by John is the climax of the novel. John's growing revulsion against everything in the World State finally propels him into a direct confrontation with it, and the authorities are forced to intervene. The events that immediately precede the riot reveal the conflicting forces that culminate in John's outburst.

John's struggle with his physical desires, first introduced on the Reservation, continues when Lenina tries to seduce him. He insists on seeing Lenina as a pure, virginal woman, possessed of complete sexual modesty. To John, Lenina is only an abstract rendering of all the virtuous women he has read about in Shakespeare's works. He struggles with the physical side of sexuality to the point that he wants to repress it entirely. When Lenina makes a pass at him, he calls her a whore for breaking the rules of a moral code she is not even aware of. "Whore" is the only other category that he has to understand Lenina. It is significant that when he locks himself away from Lenina, he chooses to read *Othello,* a play about the doomed relationship between a black African man and a white Venetian woman. Like John, Othello veers between the extremes of perceiving his beloved as a chaste statue and as a whore. It is this misperception that leads Othello to slaughter his wife, not an incompatibility between their two cultures.

John's experience in the Hospital for the Dying demonstrates the dehumanizing logic that the World State applies to death experience. Any tolerance he might once have felt for the practices and people of the World State disappears. He thinks of the Bokanovsky twins as maggots who defile his grieving process. Unfortunately for John, his mother is no help. Drugged on *soma,* she mistakes him for Popé. John's fury and agony reflects the growing anguish he experiences when he is not recognized in the World State, even by his own mother. The society of the World State names him "the Savage," associating him with a set of stereotypical characteristics. When John visits Eton, he watches a group of children laughing at "savages" on a Reservation performing ceremonial self-flagellation purification rituals. He sees himself reflected in their laughter as a curious, comedic spectacle, not as a human being. Bernard uses John as a curious specimen of "savagery" to attract important people into his own social circle. Helmholtz's laughter at *Romeo and Juliet* makes John recognize that his struggle with his physical attraction for Lenina is a comedic, offensive spectacle even for one of the World State's few nonconformists. Worse yet is the fact that he considers Helmholtz a friend with whom he can discuss his feelings for Lenina. The end result of all these separate episodes is that John acknowledges that he, as an individual, cannot exist within World State society. He is forced either to be a stereotyped representative of "the savage" or to succumb to the warped morals of the World State.

John's attempt to stir the Delta workers into rebellion by throwing away their *soma* symbolizes his struggle against happiness as the ultimate goal. John would rather see truth and real human relationships—even painful ones—than the near-slavery of *soma.* His own mother's death by *soma* is also a contributing factor. Linda and the Deltas use *soma* to escape all pain and responsibility. This makes them become infantile, something that John points out when he asks the Deltas why they want to be "babies . . . mewling and puking." John's outcry describes the essential logic that produces the "stability" that the World State loves so much. The vast majority of World State citizens remain childlike their whole lives through the use of conditioning, social reinforcement, and *soma*.

Helmholtz throws himself into the fray when he and Bernard arrive at the hospital, but Bernard hesitates. His hesitation is caused by the conflict between his desire to fit into the World State social machine and his desire to change the way it works. He fears associating himself with the nonconforming blasphemy of John's revolutionary cry and Helmholtz's support of John's actions. Bernard knows that his participation will forever mark him as a dangerous subversive.

CHAPTER 16

SUMMARY: CHAPTER 16

The police leave Bernard, Helmholtz, and John in Mond's office. Mond arrives and says to John, "So you don't much like civilization, Mr. Savage." John concedes, but admits that he does like some things, such as the constant sound of music. Mond responds with a quote from Shakespeare's *The Tempest*: "Sometimes a thousand twangling instruments will hum about my ears and sometimes voices." John is pleasantly surprised to find that Mond has read Shakespeare.

Mond points out that Shakespeare is a forbidden text. In response to John's questioning, he explains that such literature is banned for a number of reasons. In the first place, beautiful things, such as great literature, tend to last. People continue to like them even when they become quite old. A society based on consumerism, such as the World State, needs citizens who want new things. Newness is thus more important than intrinsic value, and high art must be suppressed to make room for the new. In the second place, the citizens of the World State would not be able to understand Shakespeare, because the stories he writes are based on experiences and passions that do not exist in the World State. Grand struggles and overpowering emotions have been sacrificed in favor of social stability. They have been replaced by what Mond calls "happiness," by which he means the infantile gratification of appetites.

John is inclined to think that this brand of happiness creates monstrous and repulsive human beings. He challenges the Director, asking whether the citizens couldn't at least all be created as Alphas. Mond replies that the World State has to have citizens who will be happy performing the functions that they have been assigned, and since Alphas are only happy doing Alpha (i.e. intellectual) work, the vast majority of the population actually has to be degraded and made stupid so that they will be happy with their place in life. He points to an experiment in which an entire island was populated with Alphas, and wholesale civil war quickly ensued, because none of the citizens were ever happy with the distribution of tasks.

Although the World State is a technotopia, meaning that it is made possible by technologies vastly more advanced than our own, Mond explains that even technology has to be kept under rigorous controls for the happy and stable society to be possible. Past a certain point, even labor-saving technologies have had to be suppressed to maintain a balance between labor and leisure. Keeping citizens happy requires keeping them at work for a certain amount of time.

Science has also had to be suppressed to create the happy and stable society. This is particularly ironic because World State citizens are taught to revere science as one of their most fundamental values. However, none of them—not even Alphas such as Helmholtz and Bernard—actually possess any scientific training, so they really don't even know what science is. Mond doesn't explain what it is, although he alludes to his own career as a young scientist who got himself into trouble by challenging conventional wisdom. One can infer that by "science," Mond means the search for knowledge by means of the experimental method. Science cannot exist in the World State because the search for "truth" conflicts with happiness. This is very suggestive, because it implies that the entire society is somehow built upon lies, but he is tantalizingly unclear about what truths and what lies he is talking about.

Mond tells Helmholtz and Bernard that they will be exiled. Bernard begins to beg and plead for Mond to change his sentence. Three men drag him away to sedate him with *soma*. Mond says that Bernard does not know that exile is actually a reward. The islands are full of the most interesting people in the world, individuals who did not fit in the World State community. Mond tells Helmholtz that he almost envies him. Helmholtz asks why, if he is so envious, he did not choose exile when he was offered the choice. Mond explains that he prefers the work he does in managing the happiness of others.

Mond believes that the islands are a good thing to have around since dissidents like Helmholtz and Bernard would probably have to be killed if they could not be exiled. He asks Helmholtz if he would like to go to a tropical island. Helmholtz says that he would prefer an island with a bad climate since it might help him write. He accepts Mond's suggestion that he go to the Falkland Islands.

ANALYSIS: CHAPTER 16

The conversation between Mond and John is the intellectual heart of *Brave New World*. It is here that the issues implied by the rest of the novel are made explicit, and discussed in an abstract form.

The rationale that Mond provides for suppressing John's beloved Shakespeare gives us a crucial key to understanding the rest of their conversation. The mere fact that Shakespeare is old means that he doesn't contribute to consumer behavior. (Huxley, of course, ignores the fact that people purchase new editions of Shakespeare, Shakespeare college courses, SparkNotes, etc.) While this reason seems superficial in comparison with Mond's more developed arguments, it draws our attention to the fact that consumerism is central to the world of *Brave New World*. Like other dystopias, this novel doesn't simply show us a world that is different from our own, it shows us a world that is a mirror of ours, with the worst features of our world drawn out and exaggerated. One of the central facets of Huxley's novel is directed against the ever-increasing value it places on consumerism.

By showing a world that suppresses institutions and experiences that are sacred in our own world in order to make way for the development of consumer values, Huxley demonstrates a conflict of values that exists in our own society. The "value" that drives the consumer is simply the gratification of appetites. In *Brave New World*, this one value has been developed to the point that people are "adults during worktime," but infants in their leisure time and in their relationships. So Huxley's first criticism of consumerism is that it is infantile—adults should be capable of other things.

If consumption is the "happiness" that Mond refers to in his description of the World State, the other value that his society is predicated on is "stability." In Mond's account, happiness and stability depend upon one another. The stability Mond is talking about is economic stability, the uninterrupted cycle of production and consumption. But emotional, psychological, and social stability are also important, because they all contribute to the first kind of stability.

Mond's argument about the things that must be sacrificed to create a "stable and happy" society may be read, ironically, as an argument that our values are incompatible with consumer behavior and economic stability. The values that Mond sacrifices may be summarized as follows:

FEELINGS, PASSIONS, COMMITMENTS, AND RELATIONSHIPS. Citizens of the World State have no fathers, mothers, husbands, wives, children, or lovers, because such relationships produce emotional (and therefore social) instability, strife, and unhappiness. While it is easy to think of ways that relationships make people unhappy, it may be difficult for the reader to understand why Mond thinks these relationships fundamentally create instability, when common sense and tradition dictate exactly the opposite, that the family is one of the stabilizing institutions of our society. One answer may be found in Chapter 3, in Mond's lecture to the students. Here he argues that the most dangerous part of passionate commitments to other individuals is the strength of the feeling involved. Moreover, he maintains that all feelings and passions arise from arrested impulses, such as the longing one experiences when one can't immediately have the lover that one wants. This is probably the basis for his idea that the consumer's need for immediate gratification is at odds with long-term human commitments.

EQUALITY. Mond is quite forthright about the fact that social stability depends upon inequality. Most of society is going to have to perform uninteresting tasks most of the time. This feature of World State society is by no means peculiar to the World State. In fact, it is probably true of every society that has ever existed. It might even be possible to argue that our own society has as much inequality as the World State, and that Mond is just more honest about it, refusing to pay lip service to the ideal that all humans are created equal. However, the complete abandonment of the ideal of equality leads to horrifying results. The majority of human embryos in the World State are altered so that their potential for excellence or growth is stunted. When the comparison is made between the novel's world and our own, we are left with troubling questions rather than distinct conclusions. Given that economic and social stability depends upon an unequal distribution of labor, does this create destructive contradictions with our democratic ideal that individuals are equal? (This theme is clearly indebted to the writing of Karl Marx, whose ideas are part of the intellectual background of this novel. It is no accident, for instance, that the dissident Bernard's last name is Marx.)

TRUTH. Mond says that science has to be suppressed because a society that is predicated on the search for happiness cannot also be committed to truth. He may mean that science, and the search for truth more generally, has an irresistible tendency to overthrow old, established ways of looking at things. Authority and conventional wisdom both contribute to the stability of society, and in the search for truth both of these are liable to come under interrogation.

ART. Art is not a consumer product, and great art draws its subject matter from feelings, passions, commitments, and relationships, which are discussed above.

One final category of experiences that are sacrificed in the world state might simply be labeled "problems." Huxley might argue that we value problems (old age, death, doubt, even suffering), because we value the responses that they produce in human beings. These Mond dismisses as the "overcompensation for misery."

One criticism that the reader might be inclined to level at Mond's entire line of argumentation is that it is self-serving. Mond is at the very top of the ruling class and enjoys exemption from the laws that he makes. One could easily dismiss everything he says on the basis that his real interest is the stability of his own position, and not the stability and happiness of his society as a whole. On the other hand, it would be a mistake to simply dismiss his argument out of hand, because it does possess considerable power and subtlety, challenging the reader to dispute it on its own terms.

CHAPTERS 17–18

SUMMARY: CHAPTER 17
As Helmholtz leaves to check on Bernard, John and Mustapha Mond continue their philosophical argument. Whereas their conversation in Chapter 16 covered human experiences and institutions that the World State has abolished, in Chapter 17 they discuss religion and religious experience, which have also been expunged from World State society. Mond shows John his collection of banned religious writings, and reads aloud long passages from the 19th-century Catholic theologian, Cardinal Newman, and from the 18th-century French philosopher, Maine de Biran, to the effect that religious sentiment is essentially a response to the threat of loss, old age, and death. Mond argues that in a prosperous, youthful society, there are no losses and therefore no need for religion. John asks Mond if it is natural to feel the existence of God. Mond responds that people believe what they have been conditioned to believe. "Providence takes its cue from men," he says.

John protests that if the people of the World State believed in God, they would not be degraded by their pleasant vices. They would have a reason for self-denial and chastity. God, John claims, is the reason for "everything noble and fine and heroic." Mond says that no one in the World State is degraded; they just live by a different set of values than John does. World State civilization does not require anyone to bear unpleasant things. If, by accident something negative occurs, *soma* is there to take away the sting. *Soma,* he says, is "Christianity without tears."

> *Christianity without tears—that's what soma is.*
> *(See* QUOTATIONS, *p.* 60)

John declares that he wants God, poetry, real danger, freedom, goodness, and sin. Mond tells him that his wishes will lead to unhappiness. John agrees but does not relinquish his wishes.

SUMMARY: CHAPTER 18

Bernard and Helmholtz say good-bye to John. Bernard apologizes for the scene in Mond's office. John asks Mond if he can go with them to the islands, but Mond refuses because he wants to continue "the experiment." Later, John chooses to seclude himself in an abandoned lighthouse in the wilderness. He plants his own garden and performs rituals of self-punishment to purge himself of the contamination of civilization.

One day, two Delta-Minus workers see John whipping himself. The next day some reporters come to interview him. John kicks one reporter and angrily demands they respect his solitude. The newspapers publish the incident and more reporters flock to John's home. He reacts to them with increasing violence. One day he thinks longingly of Lenina and rushes to whip himself. A man films the scene and releases a sensationally popular feely.

Fans of the feely soon visit John and chant, "We want the whip." As the crowd chants, Lenina steps out of a helicopter and walks toward him, arms open. John calls her a strumpet and proceeds to whip her, saying, "Oh, the flesh! . . . Kill it, kill it!" Fascinated by the spectacle, the crowd mimes his gestures, dances, and sings the hymn, "Orgy-porgy, Orgy . . ." After midnight, the helicopters leave and John collapses, "stupefied by *soma*" and the extended "frenzy of sensuality." When he awakes the next day, he remembers everything with horror. Having read about the "orgy of atonement" in the papers, a swarm of visitors descends on John's lighthouse, discovering that he has hanged himself.

ANALYSIS: CHAPTERS 17–18

Bernard and Helmholtz leave the scene, and the novel, at the beginning of Chapter 17. By being exiled to the islands, and by accepting their exile, they have lost the fight against the World State. Helmholtz may continue to struggle through his writing. That is the implication of his choice of a particularly harsh environment. But both of them are being physically transported to a location where they can cause little harm to the World State. Only John is left to criticize and debate with Mond.

The discussion of religion carries the book to its most abstract and metaphysical level, and the reader may have difficulty following the thread of the argument from Chapter 16 to Chapter 17, particularly given the long passages of quotation. However, this section goes to the heart of what is wrong with Huxley's dystopia: the fact that nobody conceives of any purpose for existence beyond the gratification of their own appetites. The passage from Newman that Mond quotes suggests that individuals feel the need for religion as they lose the sense that they are in complete control of their own lives, as they experience loss and the weakening that comes with age. The sense that one is not in control of one's life precedes the understanding that one is part of something larger (God's plan). In the World State, no one grows old or experiences loss, so no one ever arrives at religious experience.

In one sense, this can be seen as yet another criticism of consumerism. But Huxley is actually criticizing something larger than 1920s England and America, with its Ford motor cars, diamond rings, and conspicuous consumption. He's criticizing the way philosophers, economists, and social scientists have been thinking about society for almost 400 years—roughly since Shakespeare's day. Before that time, political philosophers from the ancient Greeks onward thought of civil society as serving some purpose. What that entailed varied from culture to culture. For Pericles, an ancient leader of Athens, the purpose of the polis (city-state) was to enable the small minority of free men to perform heroic exploits. In the Middle Ages, the purpose of the nation was frequently conceived as being to carry out God's plan by serving the King, his representative on Earth.

Seventeenth-century writers and philosophers such as Thomas Hobbes began to conceive of societies as governed by observable laws, such as the law of supply and demand, which could determine the behavior of large numbers of people. The models of society promoted by Hobbes, and later by the political economists, ultimately generated a sufficient understanding of economic and sociological dynamics to permit governments to effectively promote greater stability, as the government does in *Brave New World*. But these models simplify human life to the mere struggle to survive and escape starvation, and their insights come at the price of the earlier sense that human lives or societies have a greater purpose. And while the lack of a purpose, divine or otherwise, may be a serious flaw in the worldviews of sociology and economics, Huxley observes a much more dangerous tendency within them: the tendency for the government to produce more and more intervention into human life.

The meaning of the novel as a whole lies in Huxley's critique of modernity, characterized by technocratic government, social sciences dedicated to the control of society, and rampant consumerism, and the remarkable observation voiced by Mond in Chapter 3, that everything we think of as fundamentally human—love, passion, desire, art, and culture—comes about because of the experiences of loss and unsatisfied desire. It appears that the point of *Brave New World* is that modernity is developing in a direction that will ultimately change human nature itself. A world in which consumerism is developed to the extent it is in the World State, where desires are immediately gratified, in which "external secretion" is carried to the baby before it has barely begun to cry, would eradicate the most fundamental fact of human existence: its inconvenience.

But at the same time that it points to this conclusion, there are signs throughout the novel that this alteration in human nature has not yet taken place, and perhaps could never take place. Just as we are being told that there are no more jealous lovers, we meet Bernard Marx. Beneath the surface of the "free love" practiced among the higher castes lurks the specter of monogamy and violent passion. Lenina has already dated one man exclusively for far too long, and she indulges with an entire feely-going audience in a scandalous fantasy of monogamy practiced in a helicopter. Routinely, the citizens find themselves having to supplement their *soma* ration with drugs that replicate pregnancy or violent attachment. And there is the continuing problem of the dissidents who have to be exiled.

The last section of the novel consists of John's departure to the lighthouse to punish himself. His self-flagellation is a desperate attempt to hold onto his own values—truth over happiness among others—in the face of overwhelming pressure from the world around him. Lenina Crowne symbolizes that pressure. John feels a powerful sexual attraction to her, a temptation to give in to the "pleasant vices" that he finds so loathsome and prevalent in World State society. When she arrives along with the chanting crowd, his resolve collapses and, when he wakes the next morning, his realization that he has succumbed to the very thing he was most set against drives him to kill himself.

The language of these chapters continues in the same tone as in the rest of the book: it is a mixture, at times awkward, of didacticism, satire, and farce. The later chapters have a more serious and didactic tone, particularly in the conversation between John and Mustapha, when issues of free will, morality, God, and society come to the fore. In the last chapter, John's frantic self-flagellation contrasts with the superficiality of the gawking reporters and crowds that come to watch him at the lighthouse. The comparison between the two groups symbolizes the basic difference between John and the society in which he finds himself.

Important Quotations Explained

1.   Mother, monogamy, romance. High spurts the fountain; fierce and foamy the wild jet. The urge has but a single outlet. My love, my baby. No wonder those poor pre-moderns were mad and wicked and miserable. Their world didn't allow them to take things easily, didn't allow them to be sane, virtuous, happy. What with mothers and lovers, what with the prohibitions they were not conditioned to obey, what with the temptations and the lonely remorses, what with all the diseases and the endless isolating pain, what with the uncertainties and the poverty—they were forced to feel strongly. And feeling strongly (and strongly, what was more, in solitude, in hopelessly individual isolation), how could they be stable?

This passage comes from Chapter 3, when Mustapha Mond is explaining the history of the World State to the group of boys touring the Hatchery. "Mother, monogamy, romance" can be seen as a concise summary of exactly the issues with which John will be most concerned. And "feeling strongly" is what John values most highly, and also what leads to his eventual self-flagellation, insanity, and suicide. Mustapha is saying that by doing away with these things, the World State has finally brought stability and peace to humanity. John's critique of this position is that stability and peace are not worth throwing away everything that is worthwhile about life— "mother, monogamy, romance" included. Another facet of World State philosophy that is encapsulated in this quote is the idea of constructing a world in which human beings have only one way of behaving. The World State is an enormous system of production and consumption in which humans are turned into machines for further production and consumption. The world "allows" them to be happy by creating a system in which not being happy—by choosing truth over *soma*—is forbidden.

2. Every one works for every one else. We can't do without any
one. Even Epsilons are useful. We couldn't do without
Epsilons. Every one works for every one else. We can't do
without any one. . . .

This quotation comes from Chapter 5, when Lenina remembers
waking up as a small girl and, for the first time, hearing hypnopaedic
messages whispered into her ear. She is reminded of the quote by a
discussion with Henry Foster about the fact that all humans, regard-
less of caste, become equal after death. This quote illustrates the
power of mind-numbing repetitiveness of the hypnopaedic rules
and beliefs that form the basis of World State society. The message
also highlights the hypocrisy of the conditioning: it may be true that
"every one works for every one else," but it is also true that certain
castes have a much better time of it than others.

3. Ford, we are twelve; oh, make us one,
Like drops within the Social River;
Oh, make us now together run
As swiftly as thy shining Flivver.
. . .
Orgy-porgy, Ford and fun,
Kiss the girls and make them One.
Boys at one with girls at peace;
Orgy-porgy gives release.

This song is sung during the Solidarity Service attended by Bernard
in Chapter 5. It gives an example of the banal "religion" the World
State uses to keep its members in conformity with societal rules. The
song's silly wording helps emphasize the triviality of the ceremony.
It also contrasts with the snippets of Shakespeare that John quotes
later in the novel. The theme of anonymity is reiterated here: the
"annihilating Twelve-in-One" is a metaphor for the whole of World
State society, whose aim is to create humans that are as indistin-
guishable from each other as machines made on an assembly line.
The repeated calls to "Ford" also point out the connection to the
assembly line. Finally, the last stanza's "orgy-porgy gives release,"
like the Violent Passion Surrogate, the Pregnancy Surrogate, and
soma, is a signal that the World State has not been able to entirely
annihilate human nature. There is still some need for release, some
need to experience strong emotions that has not been entirely wiped

out through conditioning. The Solidarity Service is one of many mechanisms the World State uses to channel strong emotions in such a way that they present no threat to the power of the State.

4.   A gramme is always better than a damn . . . A gramme in time saves nine . . . One cubic centimetre cures ten gloomy sentiments . . . Everybody's happy nowadays . . . Every one works for every one else . . . When the individual feels, the community reels . . . Never put off till to-morrow the fun you can have to-day . . . Progress is lovely

These are samples of hypnopaedic sayings that are scattered throughout the novel. Lenina is a continual source of them. In Chapter 6, she responds to Bernard's soliloquy about the need to be alone with almost nothing but hypnopaedic phrases. Bernard tells her how many times, and for how long, each phrase is pumped into the ears of sleeping children. The irony is that Bernard himself is one of the people responsible for the hypnopaedic phrases, but when he tries to escape their logic he is trapped by the people around him who take every hypnopaedic saying as undeniable truth. The quotes sampled here reflect some of the basic principles of World State society: the use of *soma* to deal with unpleasant emotions; the identification of happiness as the ultimate goal; the maintenance of the caste system and the use of conditioning to create workers who enjoy their work; the prioritizing of the community over the individual; the support of instant gratification; the promotion of technology and science as necessary foundations of the good life.

QUOTATIONS

5.   And if ever, by some unlucky chance, anything unpleasant
        should somehow happen, why, there's always soma to give
        you a holiday from the facts. And there's always soma to
        calm your anger, to reconcile you to your enemies, to make
        you patient and long-suffering. In the past you could only
        accomplish these things by making a great effort and after
        years of hard moral training. Now, you swallow two or
        three half-gramme tablets, and there you are. Anybody can
        be virtuous now. You can carry at least half your morality
        about in a bottle. Christianity without tears—that's what
        soma is.

This passage comes from the conversation between Mustapha and
John in Chapter 17. Mustapha is trying to convince John that *soma*
solves one of humanity's oldest problems: it offers a way to deal
with unpleasant emotions that lead to inefficiency and conflict. He
claims that *soma* allows everyone to accomplish something that previously took years to attain. He also makes a connection between
religion and *soma*. The word "*soma*" comes from an unidentified,
probably hallucinogenic drug that was used in ancient Indian Vedic
cults as part of religious ceremonies. The *soma* of *Brave New World*
is a perversion of this ancient drug. Instead of giving insight, it
clouds over the truth. Instead of being used in solemn religious ceremonies, it is used whenever a slightly unpleasant emotion is felt.
Mustapha describes *soma* as a tool that allows everyone to be
moral, but it can also be seen as a tool that the State uses to keep its
citizens from becoming unhappy enough to try to change the society
in which they live. John rejects Mustapha's "Christianity without
tears" as being too easy, too simple, and too superficial. To John,
soma seems to be little more than an opiate of the people.

KEY FACTS

FULL TITLE
Brave New World

AUTHOR
Aldous Huxley

TYPE OF WORK
Novel

GENRE
Dystopia

LANGUAGE
English

TIME AND PLACE WRITTEN
1931, England

DATE OF FIRST PUBLICATION
1932

PUBLISHER
Chatto and Windus, London

NARRATOR
Third-person omniscient; the narrator frequently makes
passages of "objective" description sound like the speech- or
thought-patterns of a particular character, using a technique
usually called "free indirect quotation"

CLIMAX
John incites a riot in the hospital in Chapter 15

PROTAGONISTS
Bernard Marx, Helmholtz Watson, and John

ANTAGONIST
Mustapha Mond

SETTINGS (TIME)
2540 A.D.; referred to in the novel as 632 years "After Ford,"
meaning 632 years after the production of the first Model T car

SETTINGS (PLACE)
England, Savage Reservation in New Mexico

POINT OF VIEW
Narrated in the third person, primarily from the point of view of Bernard or John but also from the point of view of Lenina, Helmholtz Watson, and Mustapha Mond

FALLING ACTION
Chapter 18, in which John isolates himself in a lighthouse and punishes himself; it ends with an orgy and his suicide

TENSE
Past

FORESHADOWING
Foreshadowing does not play a significant role in the narrative

TONE
Satirical, ironic, silly, tragic, juvenile, pedantic

THEMES
The use of technology to control society, the incompatibility of happiness and truth, the dangers of an all-powerful state

MOTIFS
Alienation, sex, Shakespeare

SYMBOLS
"The bottle" as a symbol of conditioning and social predestination; *soma* as a manifestation of the use of technology to control society and the promotion of happiness over truth

KEY FACTS

Study Questions & Essay Topics

Study Questions

1. *Bernard is criticized by the Director for not acting "infantile" enough. Discuss how and why the World State infantilizes its citizens.*

The World State infantilizes its citizens by allowing them instant gratification and denying them responsibility. It assigns every citizen to a caste and a particular social function before birth, it encourages its citizens to use *soma* regularly and to seek instant sexual gratification, and it conditions its citizens to have no identity independent of the World State. John compares the dependence of Delta workers on *soma* to a prolonged childhood. Their reaction to John's call to revolution resembles a childhood temper tantrum. The lifelong process of conditioning socializes the citizens into infantile dependence on the State through the lures of pleasure, security, and happiness. Like children, they are never allowed to make independent moral choices. Instead, these choices are made for them through conditioned, blind obedience to the World State's moral laws. All of this occurs in the name of stability. Infantilization is implemented through scientific discoveries in human psychology, such as Pavlovian theory and hypnopaedia.

2.   *Discuss the relation between the sexes in the World
     State. How do men and women interact? Who holds the
     power in social situations, in the workplace, and in the
     government?*

When the Director gives his new students a tour of the Hatchery at
the beginning of *Brave New World*, it is made immediately clear that
the students are all boys. This is the first of many hints that women
occupy positions of inferior power and status in the World State.
Another clue comes soon after, when we learn that in order to retain
the State's control over reproduction, many of the female fetuses are
sterilized—but none of the male fetuses are. The Malthusian Belt,
containing regulation contraceptives, is another example of the bur-
den placed on women to avoid pregnancies. In sexual relations, men
and women seem to be equally promiscuous and equally free to ini-
tiate contact. Lenina is just as ready as Bernard to capitalize on the
fame brought through association with John by spending time with
as many partners as possible. But in work situations and in the government men are undeniably in charge. Assuming that Lenina and
Fanny are Beta females, there are very few Alpha women in the
novel and none about whom we learn anything significant. The people in positions of power—in propaganda (Bernard, Helmholtz), in
the Hatchery (the Director, Henry), and in the government (Mustapha Mond)—are all male. In the social realm the relations
between the sexes are liberalized, but in the realms of work and politics the power remains squarely in the hands of men. It is an open
question whether this state of affairs is part of the satirical target of
Brave New World or whether it simply reflects the culture in which
the novel was written.

3.   *Discuss the parallels between* BRAVE NEW WORLD *and
     Shakespeare's* THE TEMPEST.

Many critics interpret *The Tempest* as an allegory of imperialism
because Prospero decides to raise Caliban and "civilize" him.
England has a long history of colonizing "savages" it saw as being in
need of "civilizing." In some respects, the World State practices a
form of British imperialism. "Civilizing the savages" often involved
replacing native languages with English. There are hints that
English is the only language in the World State. Polish, German, and
French are referred to as "dead languages." Therefore, it seems that the

World State has eradicated most other cultures and languages except for a few "Savage Reservations." John identifies with Miranda by quoting her, and, like Miranda, he is raised in isolation from the culture of his parents. However, John resembles Caliban, because he becomes known as "the Savage" when he travels to the World State.

Bernard also parallels different characters from *The Tempest*. Like Prospero's brother, Bernard uses another person to further his own selfish interests. He uses John to acquire greater popularity and status. However, Bernard also becomes John's appointed guardian, so he becomes John's "father" on one level. Bernard's role as guardian is to expose John to "civilization." Therefore, Bernard plays Prospero, as John plays Caliban. London society's reaction to John reproduces the stereotype of the "noble Savage." This cliché often functioned as a justification for the cultural genocide practiced in British Imperialism. "Civilized" British culture played the parent role to the "child-like savage" by raising him above his "savage, childish" culture. Therefore, the relationship between Bernard and John dramatizes the thematic content of *The Tempest*, as well as the history of British imperialism.

4.   *In what ways does the World State treat people like commodities?*

The Predestinators estimate the need for various members of each caste, and the Hatchery produces human beings to match their mathematical figures. This directly follows the economic rules of supply and demand. Through the Podsnap and Bokanovsky Processes, the lower castes are mass-produced on assembly lines to satisfy the needs of a market, just like any other standardized manufactured good. Linda's doctor and Bernard are content to allow Linda to abuse *soma* even though they know it will eventually kill her. The doctor explains to John that it is better for her to die as quickly and quietly as possible now that she cannot perform any economically productive work. The doctor voices the World State's belief that human beings are things meant to be "used up until they wear out." Just as with manufactured goods, when people get old and worn out, they are thrown away. With respect to sexual pleasure, World State citizens are conditioned to view themselves, and others, as commodities to be consumed like any other manufactured good. As Bernard says, Henry and the Predestinator view Lenina as a "bit of meat," and Lenina thinks of herself "as meat."

SUGGESTED ESSAY TOPICS

1. *Discuss the relationship between science, religion, and political power in the World State.*

2. *What are Mustapha Mond's arguments against freedom? Is there any validity to them? Do you think there is a "winner" of his debate with John?*

3. *It seems undeniable that most World State members are happy, though people like John, Bernard, and Helmholtz might criticize the quality of their lives. What, then, is wrong with World State society? Discuss the relationship between truth and happiness, and the use of* SOMA?

4. *Is John really more free than the World State members? How is he conditioned in his own way?*

5. *How are the castes distinguished from each other? What is their purpose? Do you think they reflect any aspect of contemporary society or are they simply a hypothetical consequence of a society like the World State?*

QUESTIONS & ESSAYS

REVIEW & RESOURCES

QUIZ

1. What is the name of the process that allows the Hatchery to produce many clones from a single egg?

   A. The Podansky Process
   B. The Trotsky Process
   C. The Bokanovsky Process
   D. Centrifugal Bumble-puppy

2. The term for birth in the Hatchery is

   A. Social predestination
   B. Uncorking
   C. Hatching
   D. Decanting

3. How are children in the Nursery conditioned to dislike books and flowers?

   A. By preventing the children from ever seeing books or flowers
   B. By using hypnopaedia to teach them that books and flowers are worthless
   C. By spanking the children when they approach books or flowers
   D. By sounding alarms and shocking the children when they approach books or flowers

4. What two hypnopaedic lessons are the children in the Nursery learning during the boys' tour of the Hatchery?

   A. Elementary Sex and Elementary Class Consciousness
   B. Elementary Fordism and Elementary Class Consciousness
   C. Elementary Sex and Elementary Caste Structure
   D. Elementary Sex and Elementary *Soma*

5. Why does Fanny try to convince Lenina to be more promiscuous?

    A. Because she thinks Lenina is lonely
    B. Because "every one belongs to every one else"
    C. Because she thinks Henry Foster is treating Lenina poorly
    D. Because she thinks Bernard Marx is attractive

6. Why are Bernard Marx and Helmholtz Watson friends?

    A. Both feel alienated from World State society
    B. Both are committed to trying to change the World State
    C. Both have been persecuted by the World State
    D. They are friends for no particular reason

7. How does the Solidarity Service end?

    A. With singing and large doses of *soma*
    B. With an orgy
    C. With a sermon from the Community Songster
    D. With a series of hypnopaedic lessons

8. How does Bernard convince Lenina to go on a date with him?

    A. By inviting her to visit a Savage Reservation
    B. By telling her that she is "pneumatic"
    C. By telling her that he loves her
    D. She does not need to be convinced; he simply asks

9. Where is the Savage Reservation located?

    A. New Mexico
    B. Nevada
    C. Texas
    D. Arizona

10. How does Lenina react to observing the Savage religious ritual?

    A. She is horrified
    B. She is fascinated
    C. She is sympathetic
    D. She ignores it

11. Which one of the following World State sayings has to do with soma?

    A.   "Everyone is happy now"
    B.   "Progress is lovely"
    C.   "A gramme is better than a damn"
    D.   "Never put off till to-morrow the fun you can have to-day"

12. What is the purpose of the religious ritual performed by the Savages?

    A.   To bring rain
    B.   To initiate the young men of the pueblo into adulthood
    C.   To cleanse the pueblo after the outsiders' visit
    D.   To improve community cohesion

13. Why was Linda attacked by the other women of the village in the Reservation?

    A.   Because she slept with their husbands
    B.   Because she did not speak their language
    C.   Because she was from the Other Place
    D.   Because she insulted them

14. What was the first book that John read as a child?

    A.   *The Complete Works of William Shakespeare*
    B.   Milton's *Paradise Lost*
    C.   *The Chemical and Bacteriological Conditioning of the Embryo*
    D.   Orwell's *1984*

15. What is the name of the feely that John watches on his date with Lenina?

    A.   Three Weeks in a Helicopter
    B.   A Gramme a Day
    C.   A New Othello
    D.   Love in the Sky

16. After his return from the Reservation with the Savage, what event leads to Bernard's fall from social grace?

    A.   John refuses to meet Bernard's dinner guests
    B.   John tries to convince a crowd of Deltas not to take *soma*
    C.   Lenina abandons him after John refuses to sleep with her
    D.   Bernard sends Mustapha Mond a letter criticizing the World State

17. Why is Helmholtz first criticized by the World State authorities?

    A.   He writes a poem about solitude
    B.   He writes a poem criticizing the World State
    C.   He reads Shakespeare with the Savage
    D.   He spends too much time with Bernard

18. What is the lesson of the Cyprus experiment described by Mustapha Mond?

    A.   A society of Alphas is unworkable
    B.   Life on a Savage Reservation can destroy any amount of conditioning
    C.   Happiness is the only criterion for the success of society
    D.   *Soma* is a necessary component of a stable society

19. What did Mustapha Mond do that almost got him exiled to an island?

    A.   He conducted scientific experiments
    B.   He criticized the World State
    C.   He wrote poetry
    D.   He visited a Savage Reservation

20. Mustapha Mond says that "You can't have a lasting civilization without . . ."

    A.   "plenty of pleasant vices."
    B.   "*soma*."
    C.   "pre-natal conditioning."
    D.   "stability and happiness."

21. What does "V.P.S." stand for?

   A. Vigorous Panic Surrogate
   B. Viviparous Pregnancy Surrogate
   C. Violent Passion Surrogate
   D. Vivid Passion Surrogate

22. After retreating to the lighthouse, what does John do that first attracts the reporters?

   A. He cries for his mother
   B. He calls Lenina's name
   C. He whips himself
   D. He plants a garden

23. What motivates John's suicide at the end of the novel?

   A. Linda's death
   B. His unrequited love for Lenina
   C. His disillusionment with the "brave new world"
   D. His participation in a *soma*-driven orgy

24. Mustapha Mond tells John that civilizations have to choose between God and

   A. *Soma*
   B. Stability and strength
   C. Machinery and medicine and happiness
   D. Technology and progress

25. Of the following, who does not sleep with Lenina?

   A. Bernard
   B. Benito
   C. John
   D. Henry

SUGGESTIONS FOR FURTHER READING

BOOKER, M. KEITH. *The Dystopian Impulse in Modern Literature.* Westport, CT: Greenwood Publishing Group, 1994.

———. *Dytopian Literature.* Westport, CT: Greenwood Publishing Group, 1994.

DE KOSTER, KATIE. *Readings on* BRAVE NEW WORLD. San Diego, CA: Greenhaven Press, 1999.

HUXLEY, ALDOUS. BRAVE NEW WORLD *and Brave New World Revisited.* New York: HarperCollins, 1972.

———. *Island.* New York: Harper, 1962.

MOYLAN, TOM. *Scraps of the Untainted Sky: Science Fiction, Utopia, Dystopia.* Boulder, CO: Westview Press, 2000.

ORWELL, GEORGE. *1984.* New York: Knopf, 1992.

REVIEW & RESOURCES

SPARKNOTES
TEST PREPARATION
GUIDES

The SparkNotes team figured it was time to cut standardized tests down to size. We've studied the tests for you, so that SparkNotes test prep guides are:

Smarter:
Packed with critical-thinking skills and test-
taking strategies that will improve your score.

Better:
Fully up to date, covering all new features of the tests,
with study tips on every type of question.

Faster:
Our books cover exactly what you need to
know for the test. No more, no less.

SparkNotes Guide to the SAT & PSAT
SparkNotes Guide to the SAT & PSAT—Deluxe Internet Edition
SparkNotes Guide to the ACT
SparkNotes Guide to the ACT—Deluxe Internet Edition
SparkNotes Guide to the SAT II Writing
SparkNotes Guide to the SAT II U.S. History
SparkNotes Guide to the SAT II Math Ic
SparkNotes Guide to the SAT II Math IIc
SparkNotes Guide to the SAT II Biology
SparkNotes Guide to the SAT II Physics

SparkNotes Literature Guides